ENGLISH
FOR EVERYONE
JUNIOR
BEGINNER'S COURSE

FREE AUDIO
website and app

www.dkefe.com/junior/us

Authors

Thomas Booth worked for 10 years as an English teacher in Poland, Romania, and Russia. He now lives in England, where he works as an editor and English-language materials writer. He has contributed to a number of books in the *English for Everyone* series.

Ben Ffrancon Davies is a freelance writer and translator. He writes textbooks and study guides on a wide range of subjects, including ELT, music, and literature. He also works on general nonfiction books for children and adults. Ben studied Medieval and Modern Languages at the University of Oxford, and has taught English in France and Spain.

Course consultant

Susannah Reed is an experienced author and educational consultant, specializing in Primary ELT materials. She has taught in Spain and the UK and has worked in educational publishing for over 20 years, as both a publisher and a writer of ELT course books for children around the world.

Language consultant

Professor Susan Barduhn is an English-language teacher, teacher trainer, and author who has contributed to numerous publications. She has been President of the International Association of Teachers of English as a Foreign Language and an adviser to the British Council and the US State Department. She is currently a Professor at the School of International Training in Vermont.

ENGLISH FOR EVERYONE
JUNIOR
BEGINNER'S COURSE

FREE AUDIO
website and app

www.dkefe.com/junior/us

Project Editor Thomas Booth
Senior Art Editor Elaine Hewson
Editors Elizabeth Blakemore,
Sarah Edwards, Laura Sandford
Illustrator Dan Crisp
Designers / Illustrators Chrissy Barnard, Amy Child,
Shahid Mahmood, Lynne Moulding, Annabel Schick,
Kevin Sharpe, Rhys Thomas, Bianca Zambrea
Assistant Art Editor Adhithi Priya
Managing Editor Christine Stroyan
Managing Art Editor Anna Hall
Jacket Designer Surabhi Wadhwa
Jacket Design Development Manager Sophia MTT
Producer, Pre-production Robert Dunn
Senior Producer Jude Crozier
Publisher Andrew Macintyre
Art Director Karen Self
Publishing Director Jonathan Metcalf

This American Boxset Edition, 2024
First American Edition, 2020
Published in the United States by DK Publishing,
a Division of Penguin Random House LLC
1745 Broadway, 20th Floor, New York, NY 10019

Copyright © 2020, 2024
Dorling Kindersley Limited
24 25 26 27 10 9 8 7 6 5 4 3 2 1
001–340278–Jun/2024

All rights reserved.
Without limiting the rights under the copyright reserved above, no part of this publication may be reproduced, stored in or introduced into a retrieval system, or transmitted, in any form, or by any means (electronic, mechanical, photocopying, recording, or otherwise), without the prior written permission of the copyright owner. Published in Great Britain by Dorling Kindersley Limited

A catalog record for this book
is available from the Library of Congress.
Boxset ISBN 978-0-5938-4226-3
Book ISBN 978-1-4654-9230-2

DK books are available at special discounts when purchased in bulk for sales promotions, premiums, fund-raising, or educational use. For details, contact: DK Publishing Special Markets, 1745 Broadway, 20th Floor, New York, NY 10019 SpecialSales@dk.com

Printed and bound in China

www.dk.com

This book was made with Forest Stewardship Council™ certified paper – one small step in DK's commitment to a sustainable future. Learn more at www.dk.com/uk/information/sustainability

Contents

About the course	6
1 My friends	10
2 At school	16
3 Our classroom	22
4 My things	28
5 Our favorite animals	38
6 This is my family	48
7 This is my room	58
8 Review: This is me	68
9 At the fair	70
10 Our pets	78

11	My body	88
12	Our town	98
13	My home	108
14	Review: Where I live	118
15	On the farm	120
16	Sports	130
17	At the food market	142
18	At the toy store	152
19	Our hobbies	162
20	Review: What I like	170

21	Our party clothes	172
22	Our day at the beach	182
23	Lunchtime	190
24	At the park	200
25	My day	208
26	Review: Me and my day	220

The alphabet	222
Handwriting guide	223
Grammar guide	228
Answers	234
Grammar index	249
Word list	250

About the course

English for Everyone Junior: Beginner's Course is an entry-level English course for children. The course is divided into 26 units: 22 teaching units and 4 review units. There is audio for all the units.

Our characters
A group of six friends—Maria, Sofia, Ben, Andy, Sara, and Max—help present new language in a natural and friendly way.

Unit structure

Each teaching unit starts with a scene that shows new vocabulary, followed by vocabulary exercises. The child then studies and practices three or four grammar rules.

1 New vocabulary
An illustrated scene presents vocabulary in a clear context. The child listens to and repeats each new word in turn.

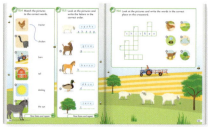

2 Vocabulary practice
All new vocabulary is practiced. The child might be asked to match vocabulary to pictures or spell individual words.

3 New grammar
Most teaching units contain three grammar rules. The grammar is first explained and then practiced.

4 New grammar
More grammar is explained and practiced. Many units also have a song to practice new grammar and vocabulary.

5 New grammar
More grammar is explained and practiced. Throughout the whole unit, new vocabulary is repeated and recycled to help the child.

Audio

English for Everyone Junior: Beginner's Course features extensive supporting audio materials. Listening to and repeating the audio recordings will help the child master the pronunciation and stress patterns of English, as well as help them plant new language in their memory.

Register at www.dkefe.com/junior/us to access the audio materials for free. Each file can be played, paused, and repeated as often as you like.

All vocabulary scenes, grammar explanations, songs, and listening exercises have accompanying audio. Clicking on the corresponding number on the app will play the relevant audio file.

Most exercises have accompanying audio. After completing an exercise, the child should listen to the correct answer and then repeat it out loud.

FREE AUDIO
website and app

www.dkefe.com/junior/us

Review units

Four review units provide the child with a chance to read a text incorporating vocabulary and grammar from recent units in the course. The child then writes a personalized answer based on this text.

Alphabet and handwriting guide

The course includes a presentation of the English alphabet, together with a guide explaining how to form each letter. The child has space to practice the formation of each letter.

Grammar guide

The key grammar taught in the *English for Everyone Junior: Beginner's Course*, together with common verbs and useful expressions, is presented in a clear and systematic way in the Grammar guide.

Learning new vocabulary

Each unit opens with an illustrated scene showing new vocabulary. The parent or teacher should supervise the child as they listen to the audio on the website or the app and encourage them to point at and repeat each item of vocabulary.

1 First, click on the corresponding unit number (here **Unit 15**) on your screen. Then, click on the exercise number, followed by **Play all**.

2 The child hears the title of the unit, followed by a short dialogue that sets the scene. After this, the audio plays each new word in turn.

3 The audio stops for a few seconds after each new word. The child should repeat the word during this pause.

4 After listening to the full audio, the child can copy each word on the dotted line beneath it. The word can be listened to again if wished.

5 A short exercise tests some of the new words that the child has just learned.

8

Learning new grammar

New grammar is explained with the help of a simple dialogue set within an illustrated scene. The child should listen to this dialogue before going on to look more closely at the example sentences together with the teacher or parent.

① First, click on the corresponding number on your screen (here **15.7**). The child will then hear a short dialogue.

② Sentences from the dialogue are then broken down into simple parts, with new language in colored or highlighted text. Read through each sentence (and the explanation) with the child.

③ Further information about the grammar for the teacher or parent is included in the **How it works** box.

④ The child then practices the new grammar and vocabulary in an exercise. After this, they can check the answers at the back of the book and listen to (and repeat) an audio recording of each answer.

1 My friends

1.1 Listen to the children.

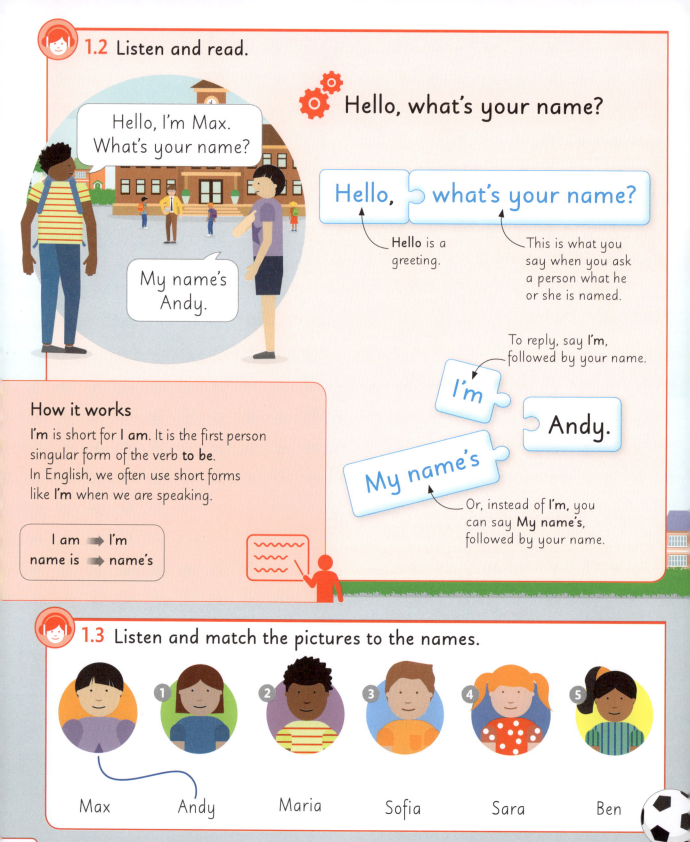

1.5 Listen, point, and repeat.

1.6 Count and write the correct numbers under the pictures.

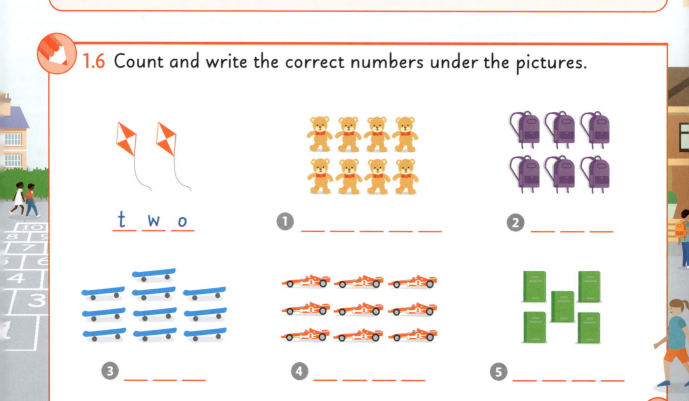

Now listen and repeat.

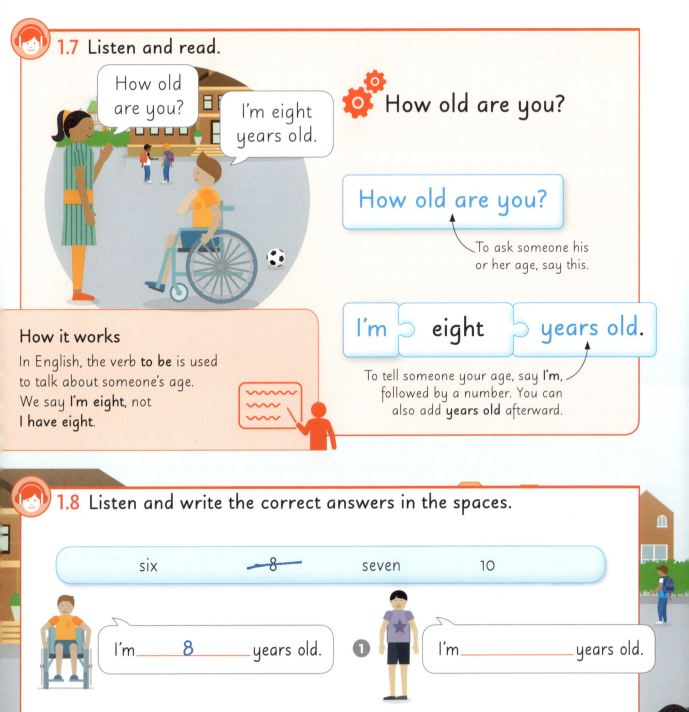

2 At school

2.1 Listen, point, and repeat.

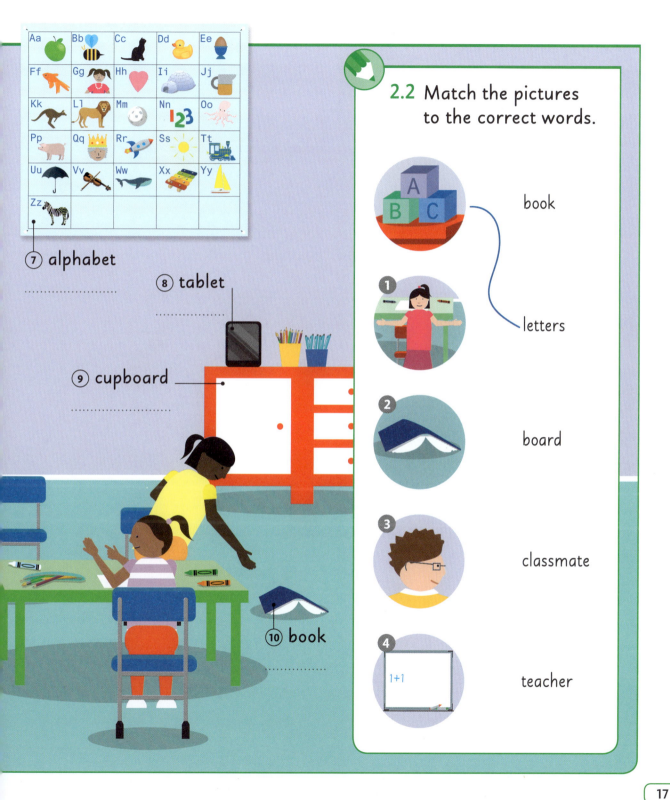

2.3 Listen, point, and repeat.

① look　　② find　　③ listen　　④ show

  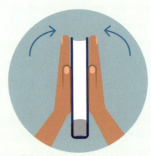 

⑤ add　　⑥ open　　⑦ close　　⑧ pick up

⑨ ask　　⑩ answer　　⑪ sit down　　⑫ stand up

2.4 Look at the pictures and circle the correct words.

(open) / close

pick up / listen

show / answer

sit down / stand up

add / listen

pick up / look

Now listen and repeat.

2.5 Listen and check off the correct pictures.

 A ☐
 B ✓

① A ☐
 B ☐

② A ☐
 B ☐

③ A ☐
 B ☐

④ A ☐
 B ☐

⑤ A ☐
 B ☐

19

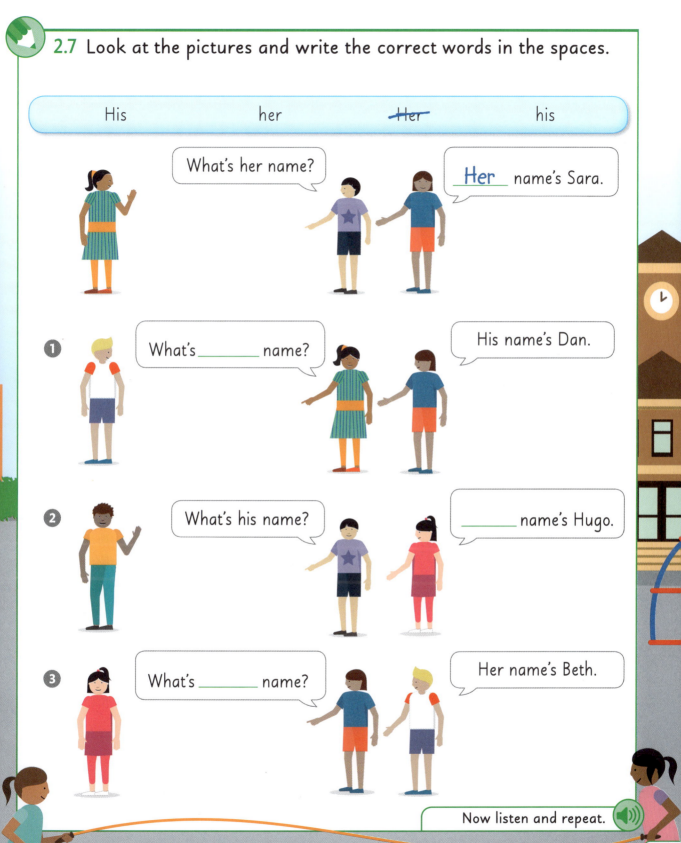

3 Our classroom

3.1 Listen, point, and repeat.

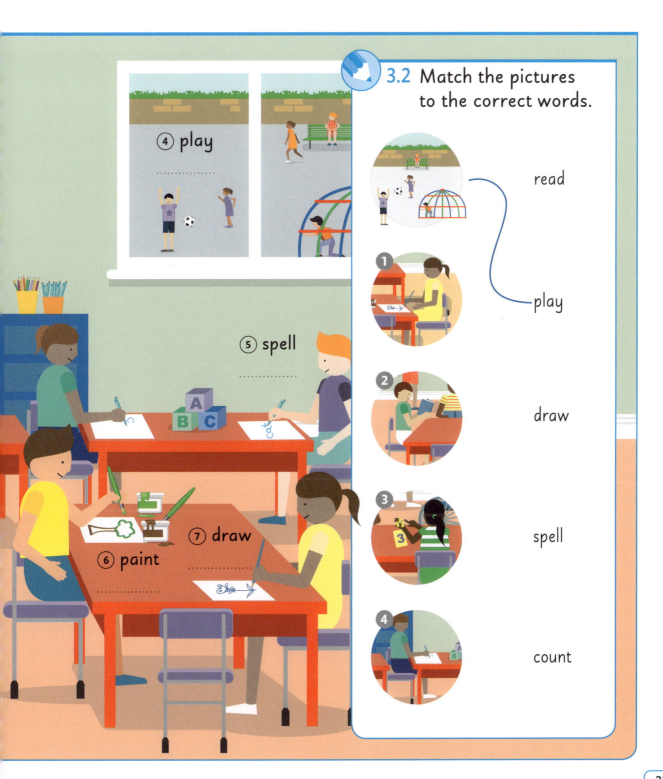

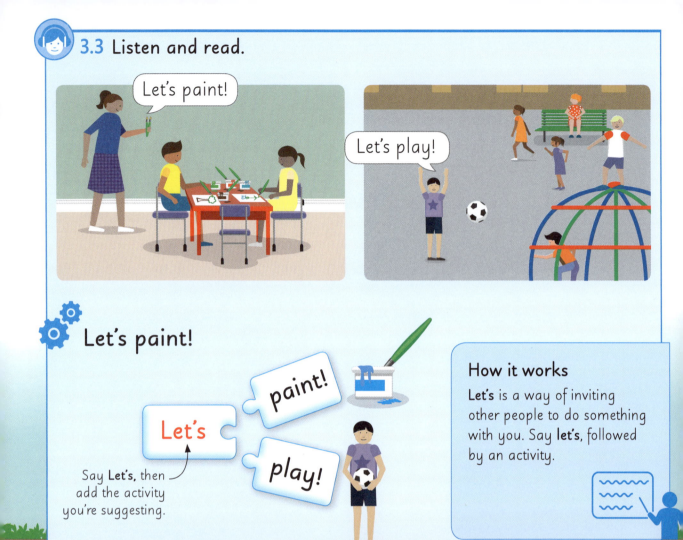

3.3 Listen and read.

Let's paint!

Let's play!

Let's paint!

Say **Let's**, then add the activity you're suggesting.

Let's paint! play!

How it works
Let's is a way of inviting other people to do something with you. Say **let's**, followed by an activity.

3.4 Listen and sing.

Hello, hello!
What's your name?
How are you?
Let's play a game.

Let's say hello
to my new friends
Max and Maria,
Sara and Ben.

3.5 Look at the pictures and check off the correct sentences.

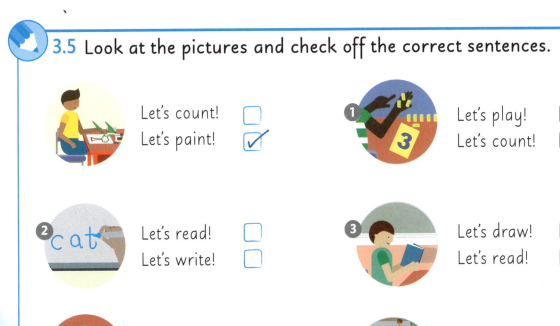

Let's count! ☐
Let's paint! ☑

1. Let's play! ☐
   Let's count! ☐

2.  Let's read! ☐
   Let's write! ☐

3. Let's draw! ☐
   Let's read! ☐

4. Let's draw! ☐
   Let's count! ☐

5. Let's play! ☐
   Let's write! ☐

Now listen and repeat.

 3.6 Listen and write the correct words in the spaces.

| write | ~~play~~ | read | count |

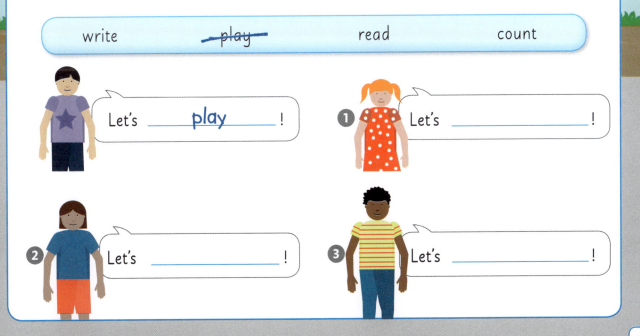

Let's ___play___ !

1. Let's _____ !

2. Let's _____ !

3. Let's _____ !

25

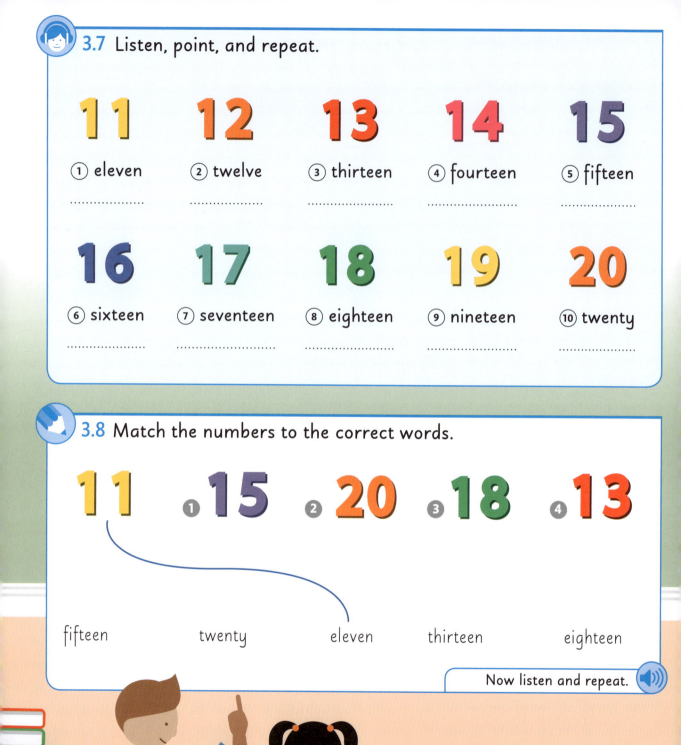

3.7 Listen, point, and repeat.

① eleven　② twelve　③ thirteen　④ fourteen　⑤ fifteen

⑥ sixteen　⑦ seventeen　⑧ eighteen　⑨ nineteen　⑩ twenty

3.8 Match the numbers to the correct words.

11　①15　②20　③18　④13

fifteen　twenty　eleven　thirteen　eighteen

Now listen and repeat.

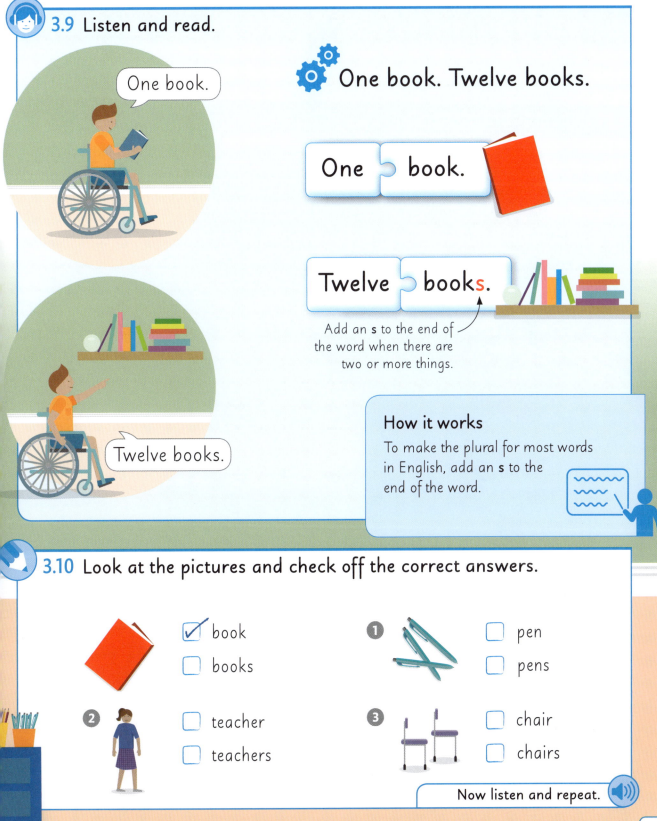

4 My things

4.1 Listen, point, and repeat.
4.2 Count the pencils.

4.3 Write the correct words next to the pictures.

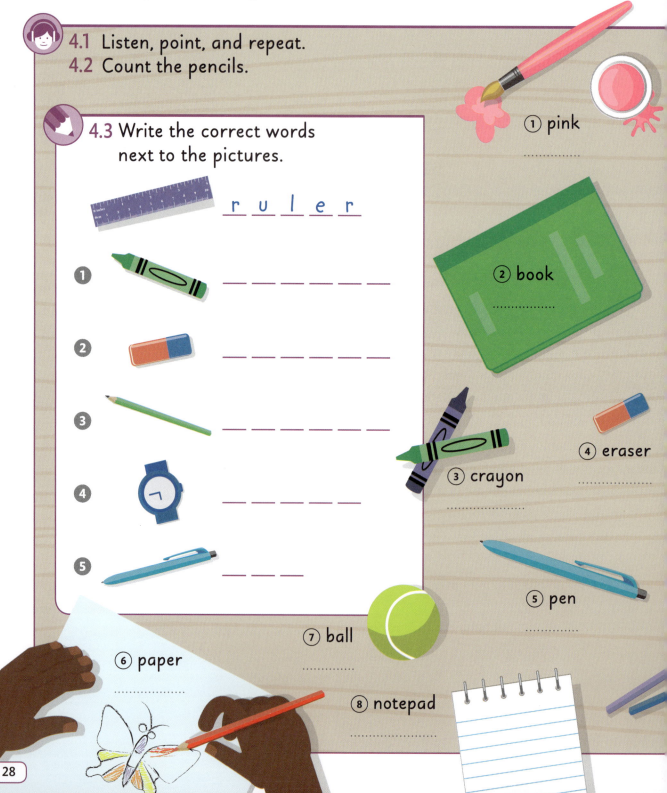

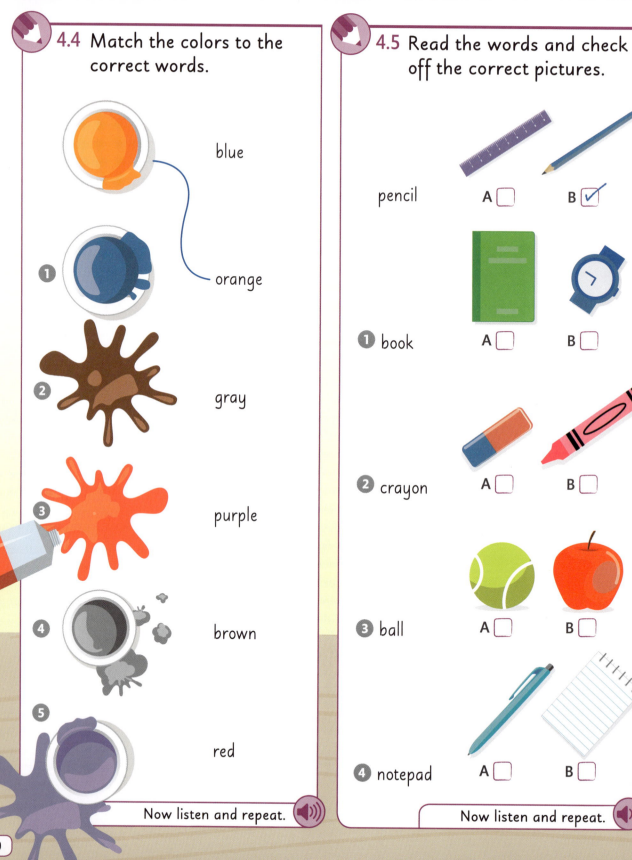

4.6 There are six words. Mark the beginning and end of each word and write them below.

yellow|crayonwhiteblackgreenapple

___yellow___ 1. _____

2. _____ 3. _____

4. _____ 5. _____

Now listen and repeat.

4.7 Listen and read.

What's this?

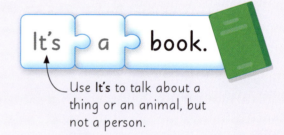

Use **It's** to talk about a thing or an animal, but not a person.

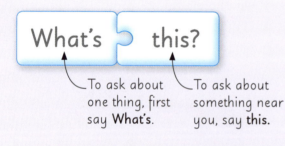

To ask about one thing, first say **What's**.

To ask about something near you, say **this**.

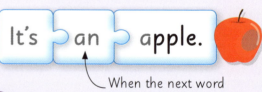

When the next word begins with **a, e, i, o,** or **u**, put **an** before it.

How it works

Ask **What's this?** when you want somebody to identify a thing that is near you. When answering, say **It's a**, followed by the thing or animal you're talking about.

What is ➡ What's
It is ➡ It's

4.8 Look at the pictures and write the correct answers in the spaces.

It's a watch.   ~~It's a book.~~   It's an apple.   It's an eraser.

It's a book.

Now listen and repeat.

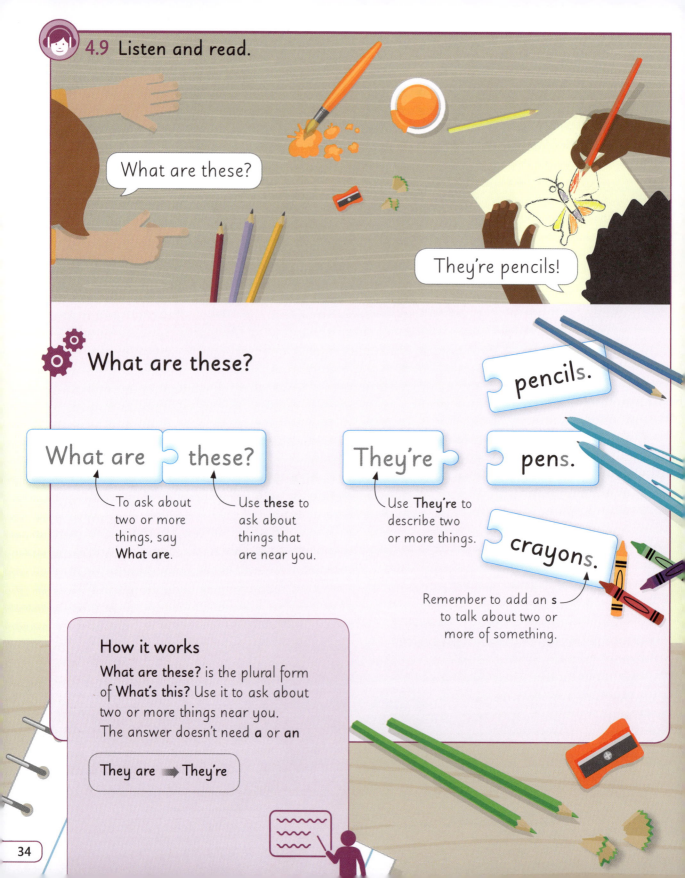

4.10 Look at the pictures and write the correct words in the spaces.

crayons ~~pencils~~ rulers erasers notepads

What are these?
They're __pencils__ .

① What are these?
They're _____ .

② What are these?
They're _____ .

③ What are these?
They're _____ .

④ What are these?
They're _____ .

Now listen and repeat.

4.11 Listen and sing.

Red, yellow, green, and blue!

Black, white, and orange, too!

4.13 Listen and color in the pictures.

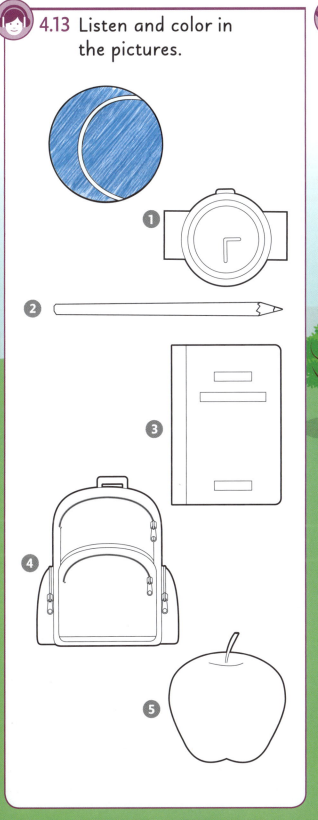

4.14 Look at the pictures and write the correct answers in the spaces.

It's black.   It's red.   ~~It's pink.~~
It's purple.   It's yellow.

What color is the crayon?
It's pink.

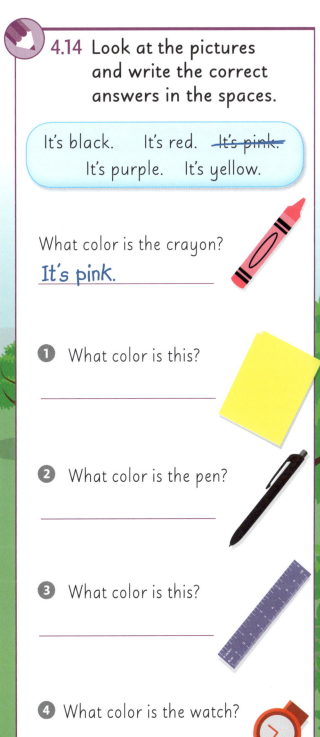

1. What color is this?
_____

2. What color is the pen?
_____

3. What color is this?
_____

4. What color is the watch?
_____

Now listen and repeat.

5 Our favorite animals

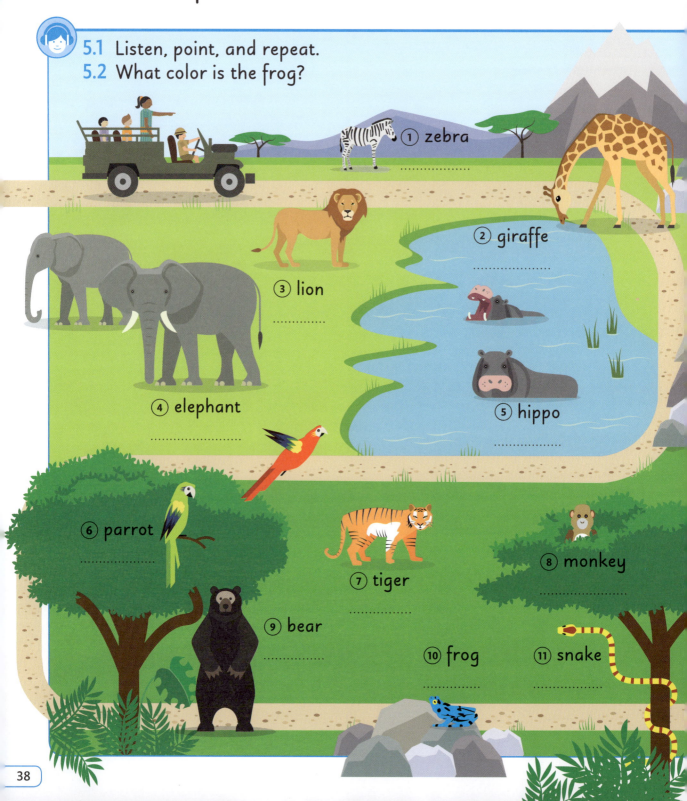

5.1 Listen, point, and repeat.
5.2 What color is the frog?

1. zebra
2. giraffe
3. lion
4. elephant
5. hippo
6. parrot
7. tiger
8. monkey
9. bear
10. frog
11. snake

5.4 Look at the pictures and check off the correct words.

snake ☐
hippo ☑
crocodile ☐

1 whale ☐
parrot ☐
crocodile ☐

2 lion ☐
bear ☐
monkey ☐

3 frog ☐
tiger ☐
giraffe ☐

Now listen and repeat.

5.5 Match the pictures to the correct words.

1  **2**  **3**  **4**

snake   zebra   lion   penguin   lizard

Now listen and repeat.

40

5.6 Listen and check off the correct pictures.

A  ☐ B ☑

1. A  ☐ B ☐
2. A  ☐ B ☐
3. A  ☐ B ☐

5.7 Listen and sing.

♪ Animals, animals everywhere! ♪
A lion, a giraffe,
and a polar bear.

♪ A whale and a penguin,
a tiger and a snake,
animals, animals,
they are great! ♪

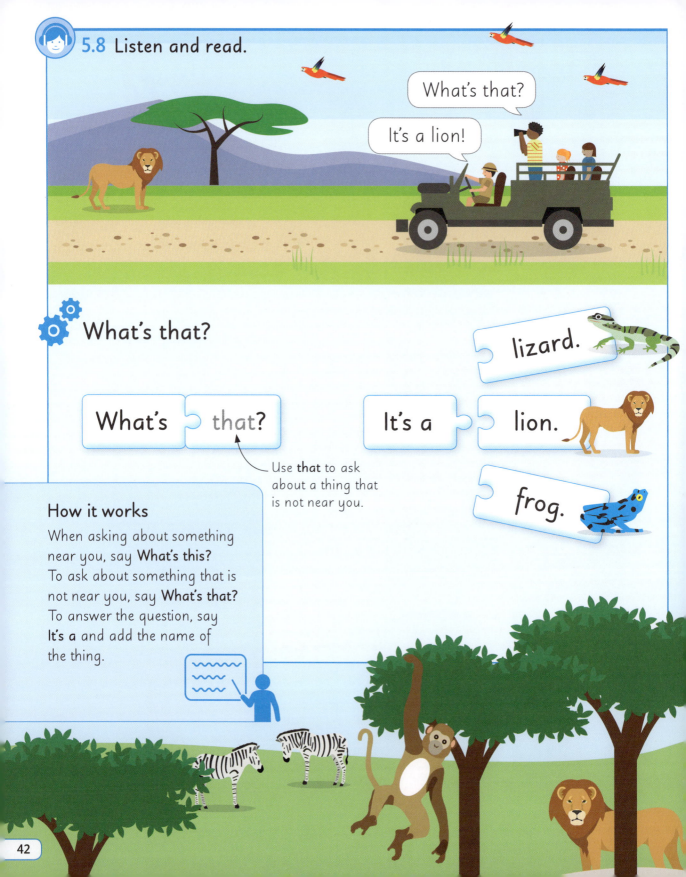

5.9 Look at the pictures and write the correct words in the spaces.

crocodile   ~~lion~~   giraffe   bear

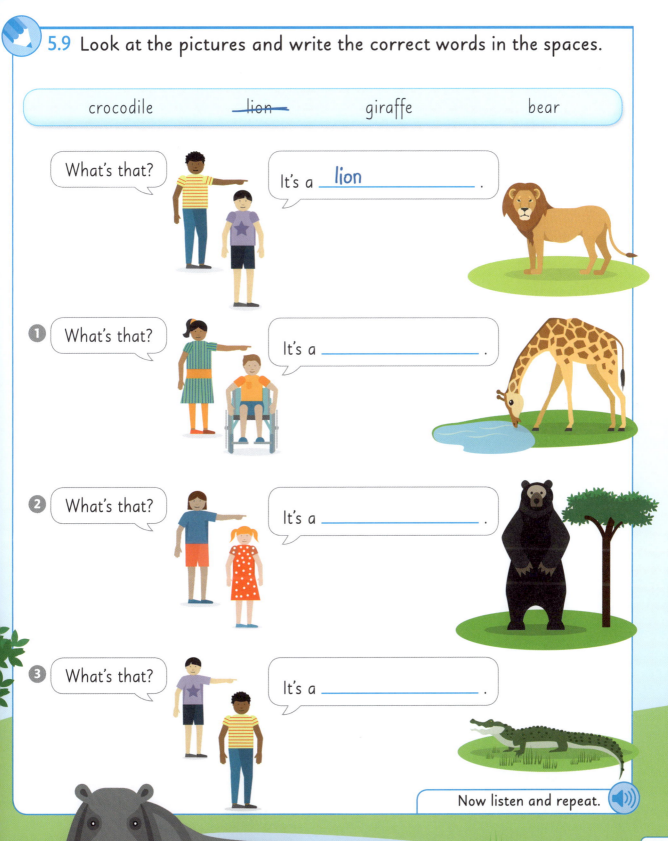

It's a __lion__.

1. It's a _____.
2. It's a _____.
3. It's a _____.

Now listen and repeat.

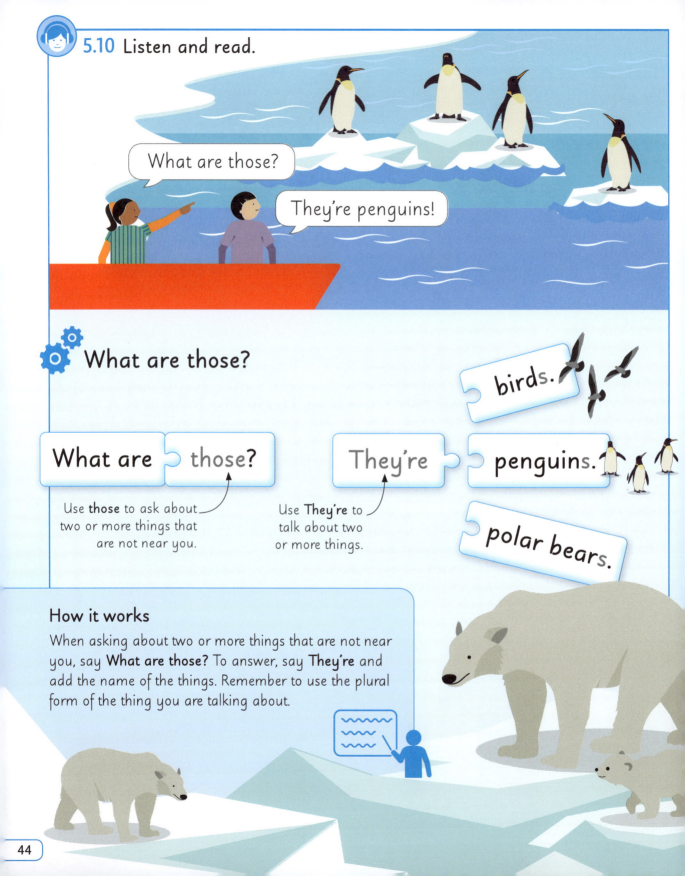

5.11 Listen and check off the correct pictures.

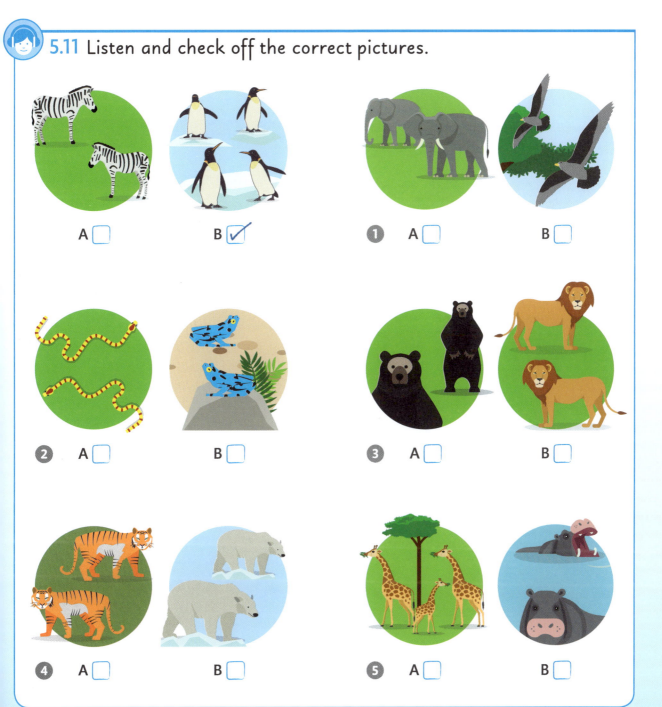

6 This is my family

6.1 Listen, point, and repeat.
6.2 Find the giraffes.

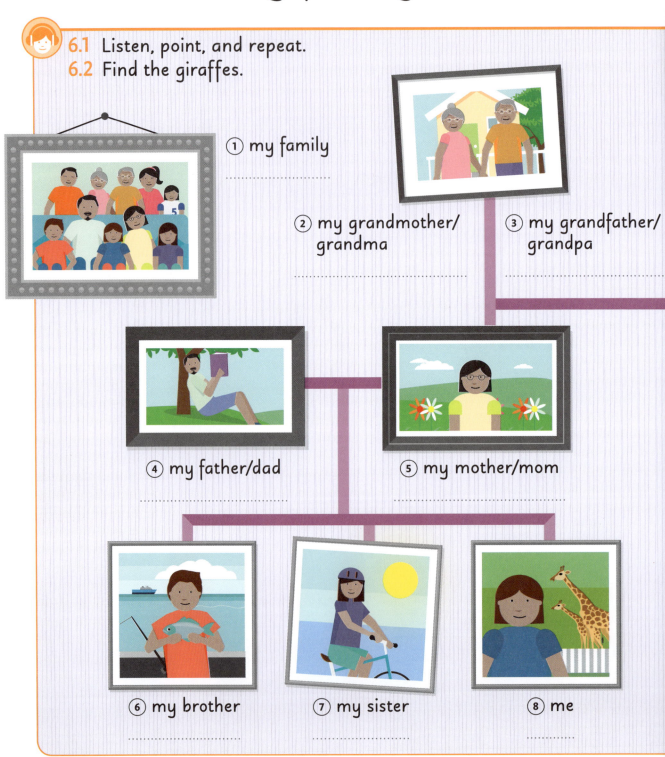

① my family
② my grandmother/grandma
③ my grandfather/grandpa
④ my father/dad
⑤ my mother/mom
⑥ my brother
⑦ my sister
⑧ me

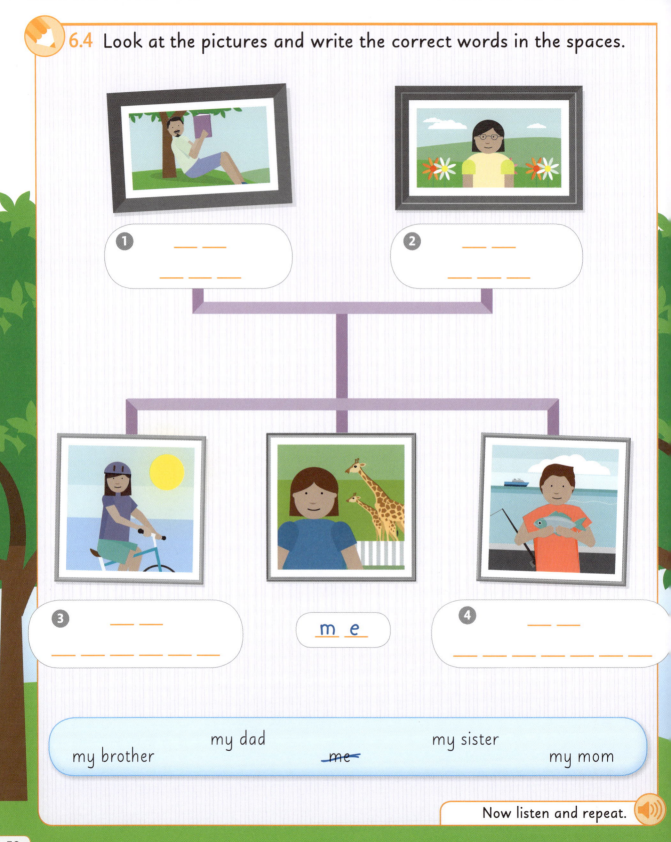

6.5 Look at the pictures and circle the correct words.

(sister) / grandfather   mother / uncle   grandma / dad

aunt / brother   mom / grandpa   grandma / father

Now listen and repeat.

6.6 Look at the pictures and write the words in the correct place on the crossword.

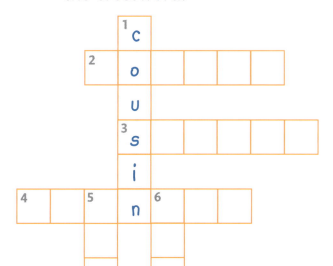

51

6.7 Listen and read.

Who's this? Who's that?

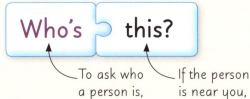

To ask who a person is, use **Who's**.

If the person is near you, use **this**.

If the person is not near you, use **that**.

To talk about a boy or man, use **He's**.

Use **my** to talk about someone who is related to you.

To talk about a girl or woman, use **She's**.

How it works

Who is the question word used to ask about people. **He's** and **She's** are third person singular forms of the verb **to be**. Use **he** to talk about males and **she** to talk about females.

Who is ➡ Who's
He is ➡ He's
She is ➡ She's

6.8 Look at the pictures and write the correct questions in the spaces.

> Who's this?   ~~Who's that?~~   Who's this?   Who's that?

Who's that?
— She's my aunt.

1. _____
— She's my mother.

2. _____
— He's my grandfather.

3. _____
— She's my sister.

Now listen and repeat.

 **6.9 Listen and read.**

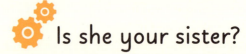 **Is she your sister?**

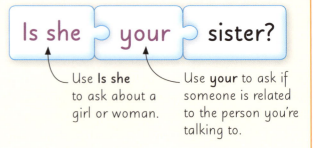
Use **Is she** to ask about a girl or woman.
Use **your** to ask if someone is related to the person you're talking to.

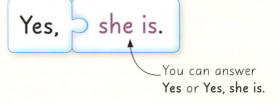
You can answer **Yes** or **Yes, she is.**

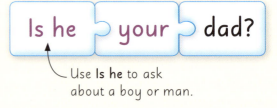
Use **Is he** to ask about a boy or man.

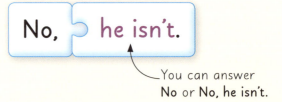
You can answer **No** or **No, he isn't.**

How it works
To ask a question using the verb **to be**, put **is** before **he** or **she**.
Your is the possessive adjective to say that something belongs to the person you're talking to.

Is not ➡ Isn't

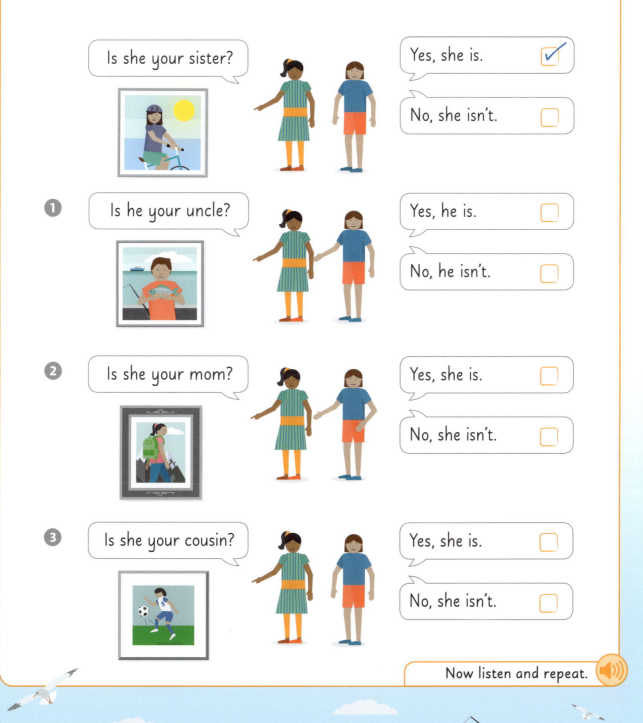

6.11 Listen, point, and repeat.

1. teacher
2. vet
3. farmer
4. doctor
5. chef
6. police officer
7. firefighter

6.12 Listen and read.

She's a teacher.

She's / He's · a · teacher.

Use *a* before the person's job.

6.13 Match the pictures to the correct jobs.

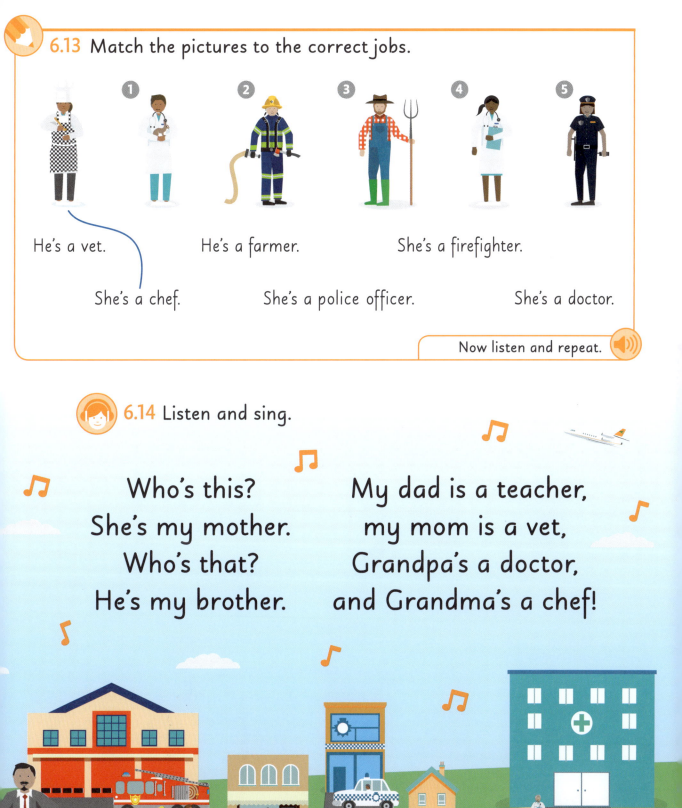

He's a vet.　　　　He's a farmer.　　　　She's a firefighter.

　　She's a chef.　　She's a police officer.　　She's a doctor.

Now listen and repeat.

6.14 Listen and sing.

Who's this?　　　　My dad is a teacher,
She's my mother.　　my mom is a vet,
Who's that?　　　　Grandpa's a doctor,
He's my brother.　　and Grandma's a chef!

7 This is my room

7.1 Listen, point, and repeat.
7.2 Find the purple car.

7.4 Match the pictures to the correct words.

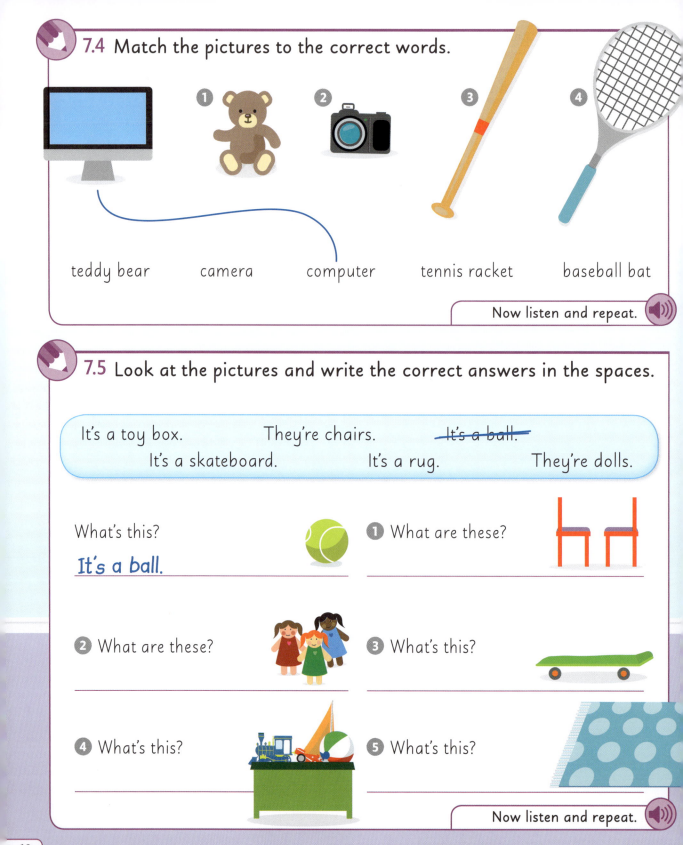

teddy bear   camera   computer   tennis racket   baseball bat

Now listen and repeat.

7.5 Look at the pictures and write the correct answers in the spaces.

It's a toy box.   They're chairs.   ~~It's a ball.~~
It's a skateboard.   It's a rug.   They're dolls.

What's this?
It's a ball.

① What are these?

② What are these?

③ What's this?

④ What's this?

⑤ What's this?

Now listen and repeat.

60

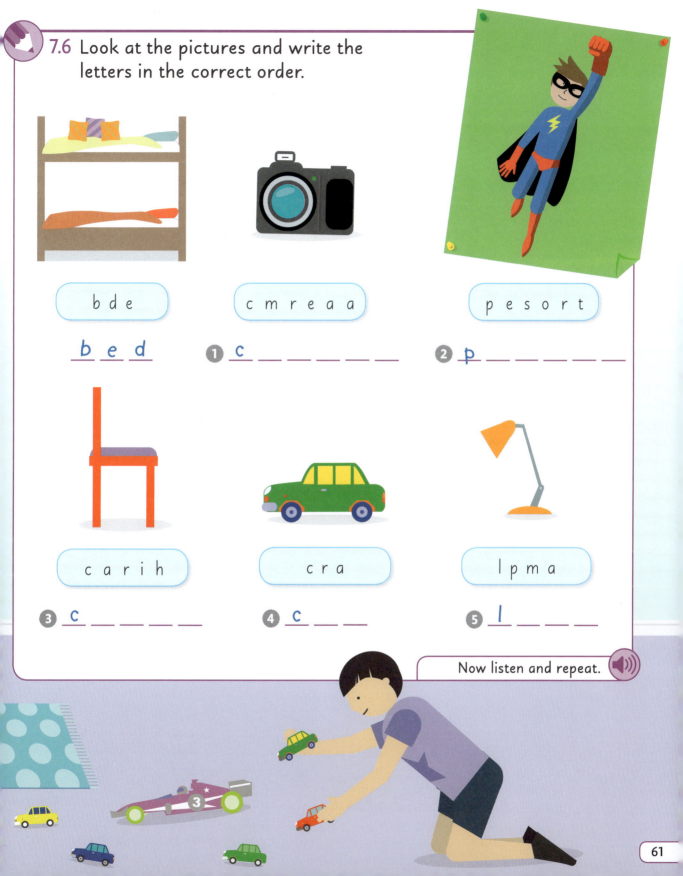

7.8 Look at the pictures and check off the correct sentences.

This is my toy box. ✓
These are my toy boxes. ☐

1. This is my doll. ☐
   These are my dolls. ☐

2. This is my lamp. ☐
   These are my lamps. ☐

3. This is my rug. ☐
   These are my rugs. ☐

Now listen and repeat. 🔊

7.9 Look at the pictures and write the correct words in the spaces.

That's   ~~Those are~~   Those are   That's

Those are my toys.

1. _____ my poster.

2. _____ my skateboard.

3. _____ my cars.

Now listen and repeat. 🔊

63

7.10 Listen and read.

⚙ I have a desk.

| I have | a desk. |

Say this to talk about things you have.

| I don't have | a desk. |

Say this to talk about things you don't have.

How it works

To talk about things you own or possess, use **I have** followed by **a** or **an**, then the item.

To talk about things you don't own or possess, use **I don't have**.

Do not ➡ Don't

7.11 Look at the pictures and write the correct names in the spaces.

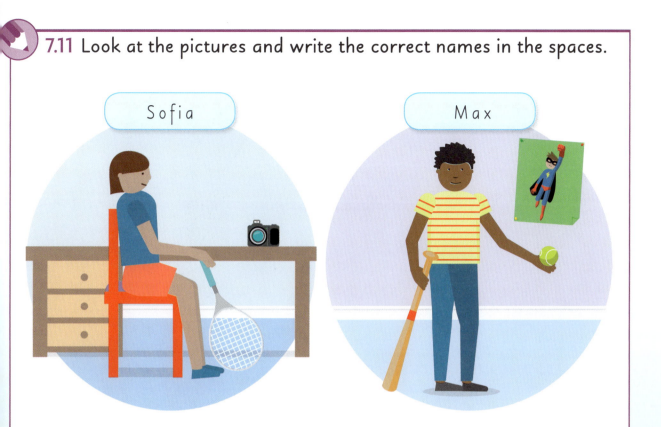

I have a desk.

__Sofia__

① I have a ball.

_____

② I don't have a chair.

_____

③ I have a tennis racket.

_____

④ I have a baseball bat.

_____

⑤ I don't have a ball.

_____

Now listen and repeat.

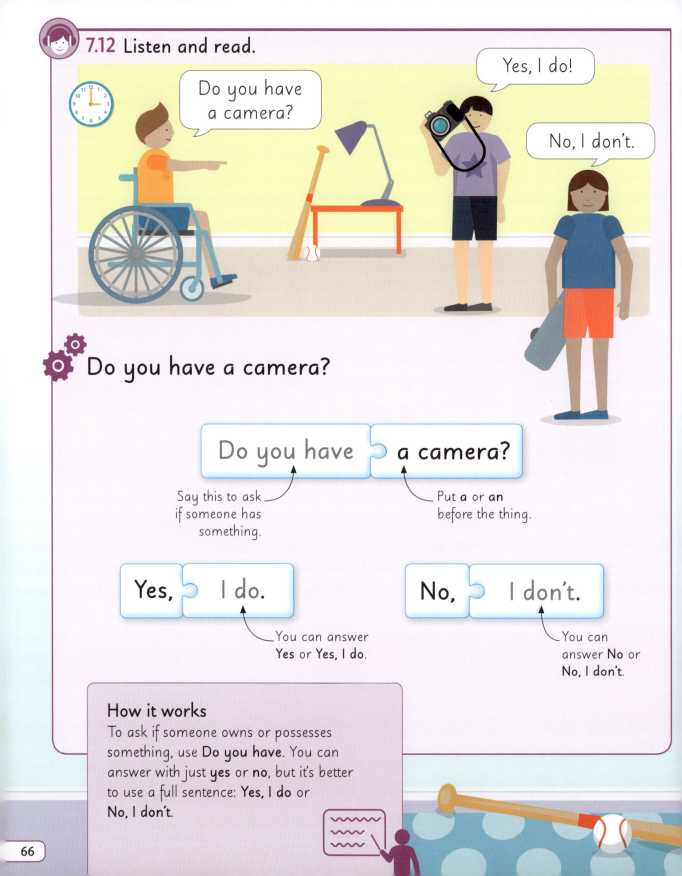

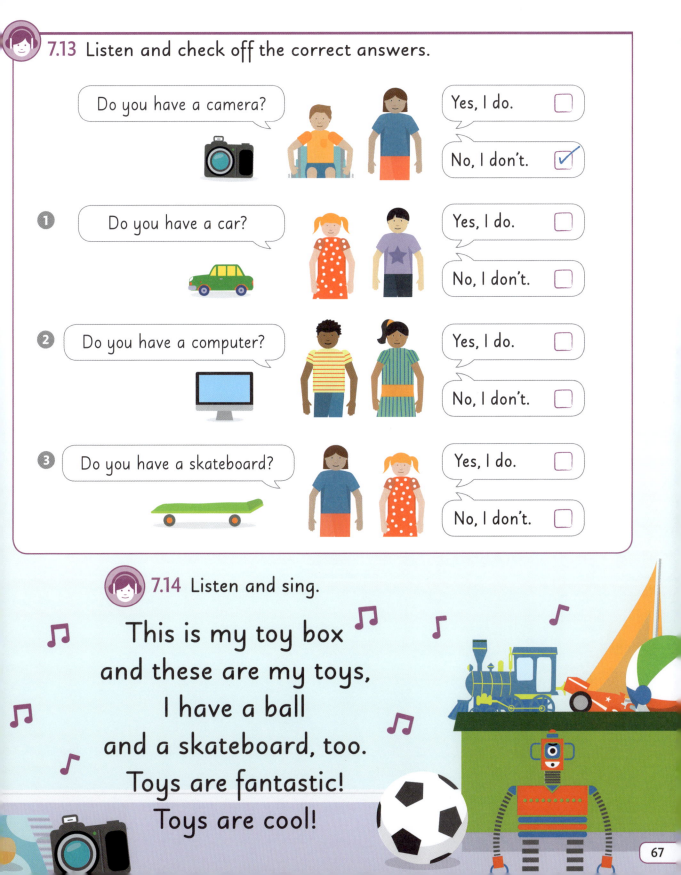

8 Review: This is me

 8.1 Listen and read.

My name's Ben.
I'm eight years old.
My favorite animal is a penguin.
My favorite color is green.
I have a tennis racket.
I don't have a baseball bat.

This is my family.

8.2 Write about yourself and draw your family.

My name's _____.
I'm _____ years old.
My favorite animal is a _____.
My favorite color is _____.
I have a _____.
I don't have a _____.

This is my family.

9.6 Look at the pictures and write the letters in the correct order.

h t o
<u>h</u> <u>o</u> <u>t</u>

h y g r u n
<u>h</u> _ _ _ _ _

h p a y p
<u>h</u> _ _ _ _

s d r a e c
<u>s</u> _ _ _ _ _

s d a
<u>s</u> _ _

t s y h t i r
<u>t</u> _ _ _ _ _

Now listen and repeat.

9.7 Listen and sing.

Are you happy?
Yes, we are!
We are at the fair.

Are you tired?
No, we aren't.
We aren't tired
or scared!

9.8 Listen and read.

We're happy!

We're happy!

To talk about a group that you're part of, use **We're**.

They're scared.

To talk about a group that doesn't include yourself or the person you're speaking to, use **They're**.

We're **really** happy!

They're **very** scared.

To say how strongly you (or other people) are feeling, put **really** or **very** before the describing word (adjective).

How it works

We're and **they're** are examples of the **present simple** of the verb **to be**.

Put an adjective after the verb **to be** to describe how you (or other people) are feeling. Putting **really** or **very** before the adjective makes it stronger.

We are ➡ We're
They are ➡ They're

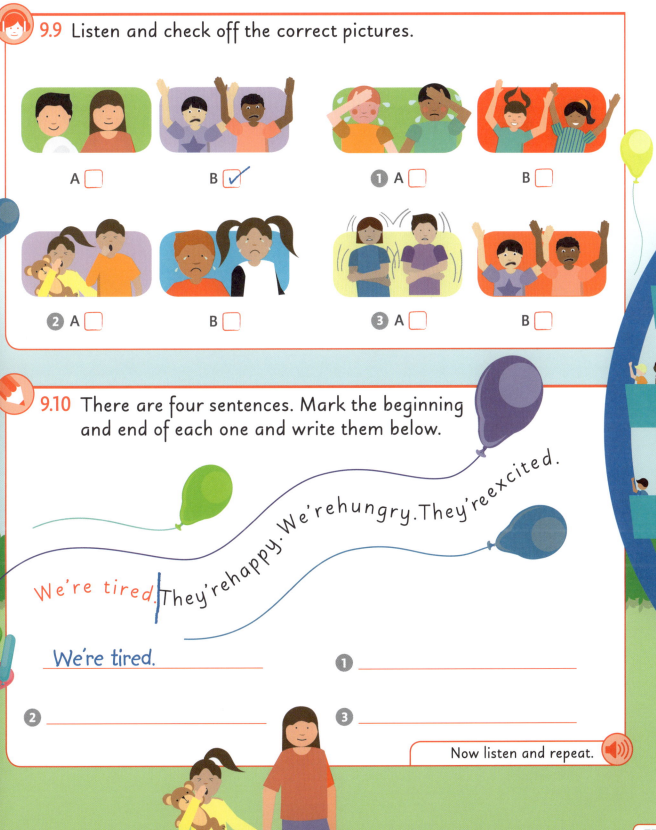

9.11 Listen and read.

Are you hungry?

Are you | **hungry?**

Are you can be used to talk to one person or a group of people.

Yes, | **we are.**

To answer on behalf of a group, say **Yes, we are** or **No, we aren't**.

No, | **we aren't.**

Are they | **sad?**

To ask about a group that you're not part of, use **Are they**.

Yes, | **they are.**

To describe a group you're not part of, say **Yes, they are** or **No, they aren't**.

No, | **they aren't.**

How it works

Are you and **Are they** are question forms of the verb **to be**.

Are not ➡ Aren't

9.12 Look at the pictures and write the correct answers in the spaces.

Yes, they are.   No, we aren't.   No, they aren't.   ~~Yes, we are.~~

Now listen and repeat.

10 Our pets

10.1 Listen, point, and repeat.
10.2 Count the fish.

10.3 Match the pictures to the correct words.

10.7 Find and circle the five words in the grid.

- cat
- vet
- ~~young~~
- rabbit
- collar
- mouse

c	r	m	a	n	d
o	y	o	u	n	g
l	s	u	v	e	g
l	c	s	e	r	c
a	y	e	t	d	a
r	a	b	b	i	t

 10.8 Listen and sing.

I have a cat,
she's black and small.
She likes to run
and play with a ball.

Maria has a tortoise,
his name is Socks.
He's old and green
and he's in this box.

10.10 Listen and match the person to the correct pet.

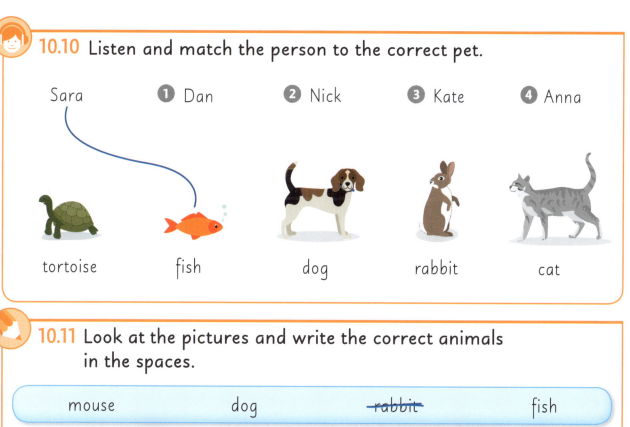

10.11 Look at the pictures and write the correct animals in the spaces.

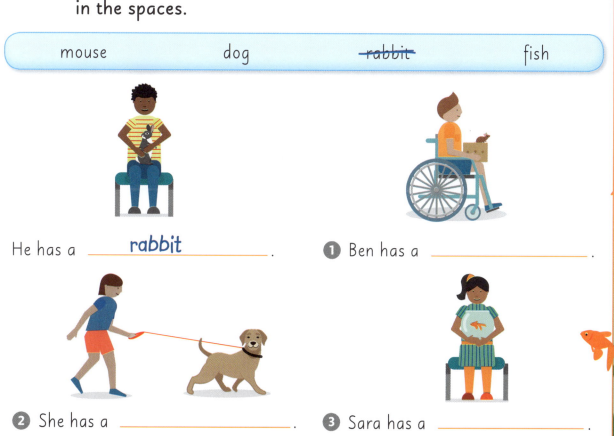

10.12 Listen and read.

Does she have a tortoise?

Does she have — **a tortoise**

Use these words to ask if a girl or woman has something.

Yes, — **she does.**

You can say **Yes** or **Yes, she does.**

Does he have — **a rabbit?**

You can also say the person's name instead of **he** or **she**.

No, — **he doesn't.**

You can say **No** or **No, he doesn't.**

How it works

To ask if someone owns or possesses something, say **Does she have** or **Does he have**, followed by the thing you're asking about.

Does not ➡ Doesn't

84

10.13 Look at the pictures and write the correct answers in the spaces.

> No, he doesn't.   ~~Yes, she does.~~   No, she doesn't.   Yes, he does.

Does she have a tortoise?

Yes, she does.

❶ Does she have a spider?

_____

❷ Does he have a mouse?

_____

❸ Does he have a rabbit?

_____

Now listen and repeat.

10.14 Listen and check off the correct pictures.

A ☐   B ✔   ❶ A ☐   B ☐

❷ A ☐   B ☐   ❸ A ☐   B ☐

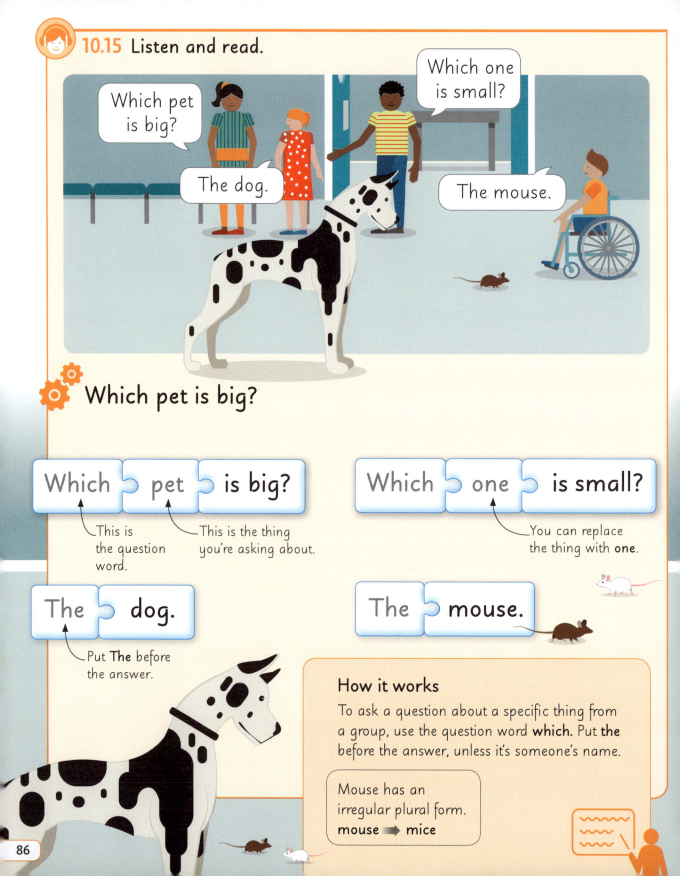

10.16 Look at the pictures and write the correct dog's name under the questions.

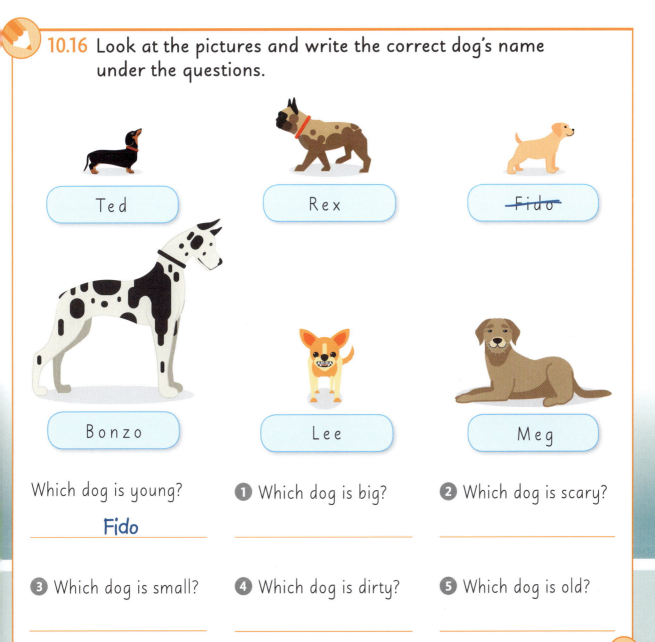

Which dog is young?
Fido

① Which dog is big?

② Which dog is scary?

③ Which dog is small?

④ Which dog is dirty?

⑤ Which dog is old?

Now listen and repeat.

I have a tortoise. Do you have a pet?

And you?

87

11 My body

11.1 Listen, point, and repeat.
11.2 Who has long hair?

11.4 Look at the pictures and check off the correct words.

nose ☐
foot ✓
hand ☐

1 arm ☐
head ☐
leg ☐

2 face ☐
fingers ☐
toes ☐

3 body ☐
eye ☐
mouth ☐

Now listen and repeat.

11.5 Look at the pictures and write the words in the correct place on the crossword.

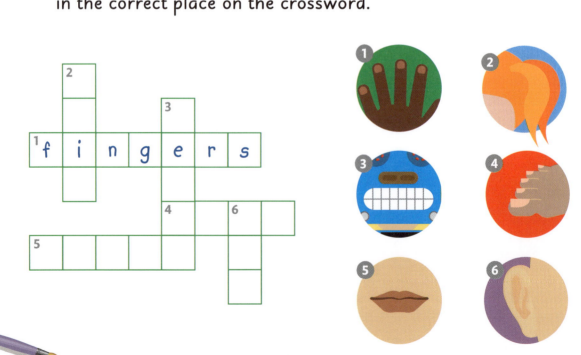

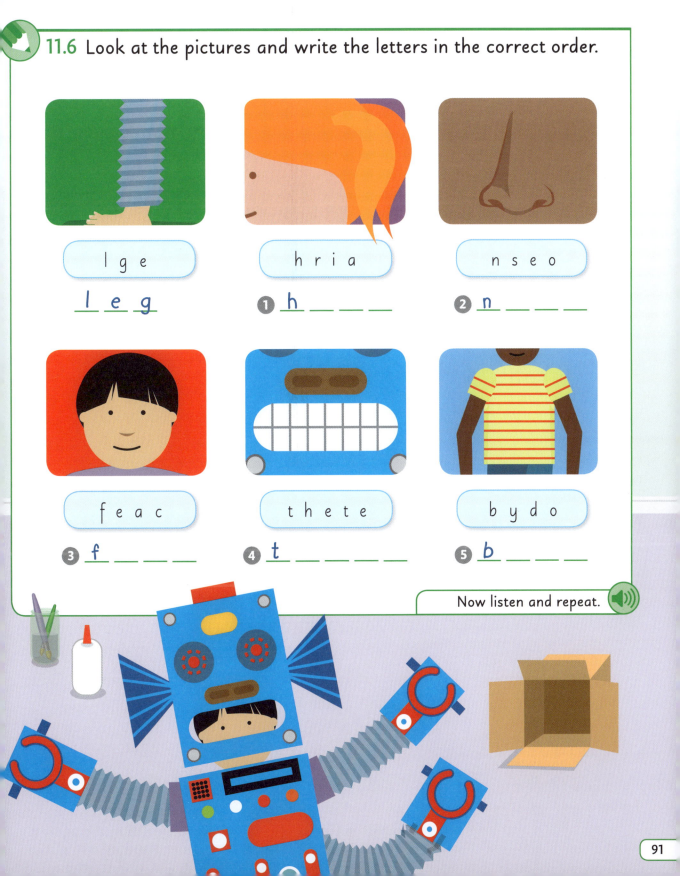

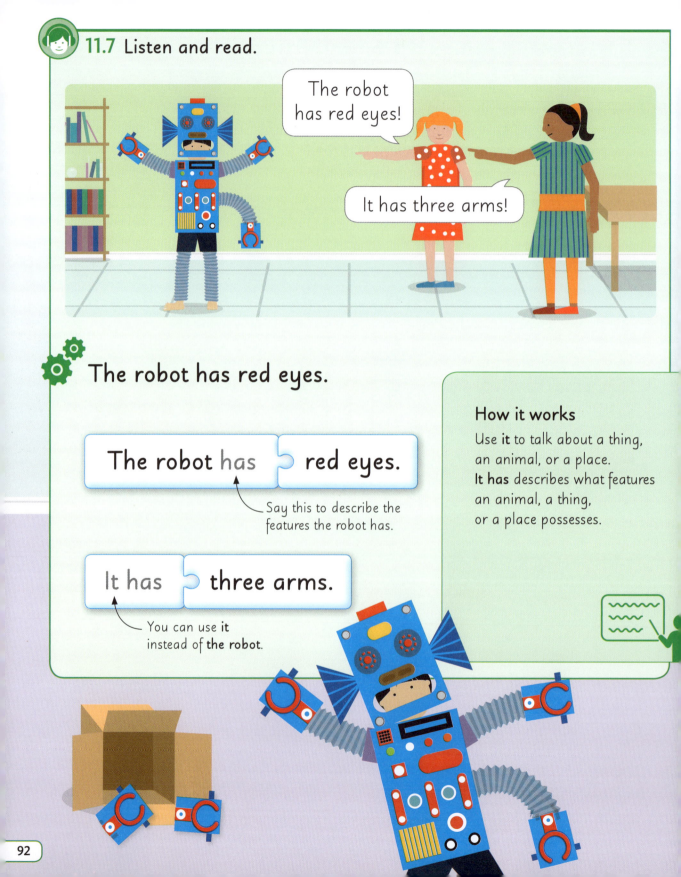

11.8 Listen and check off the correct pictures.

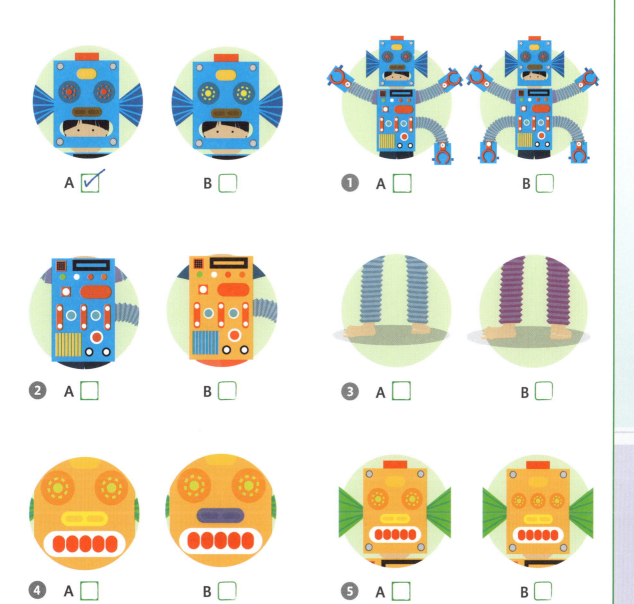

11.9 Listen and read.

Does it have blue arms?

Say this to ask what features a thing, an animal, or a place has.

You can answer
Yes or **Yes, it does**.

You can answer **No**
or **No, it doesn't**.

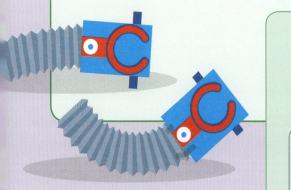

How it works

To ask if a thing, an animal, or a place possesses something, use **Does it have**, and then the feature you are asking about.

Teeth is an irregular plural.
tooth ➡ **teeth**

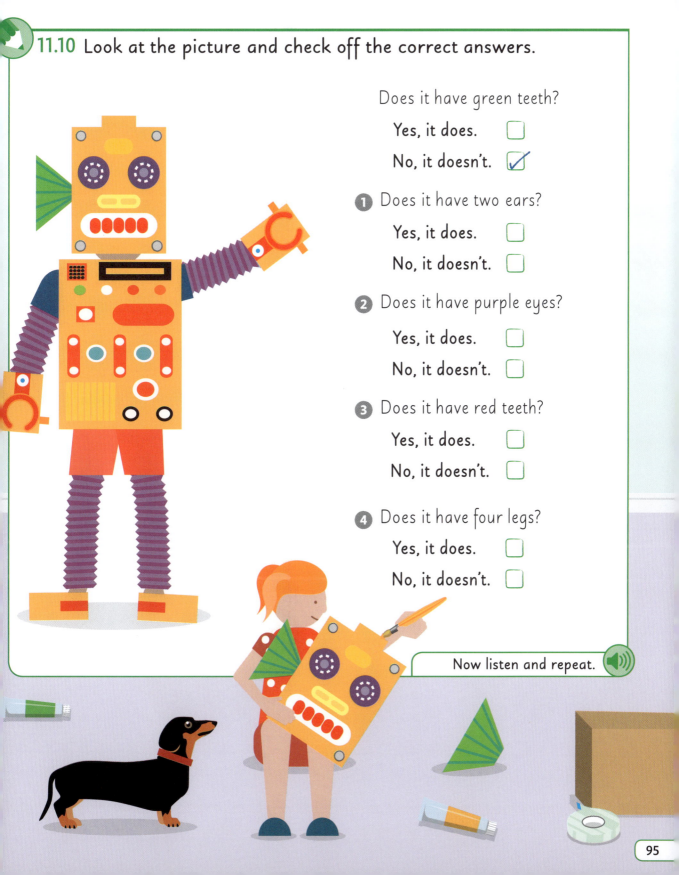

11.11 Listen, point, and repeat.

① touch　② clap　③ point　④ wave　⑤ move

11.12 Look at the pictures and write the correct words in the spaces.

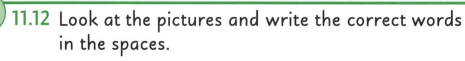

Move　~~Touch~~　Point　Wave

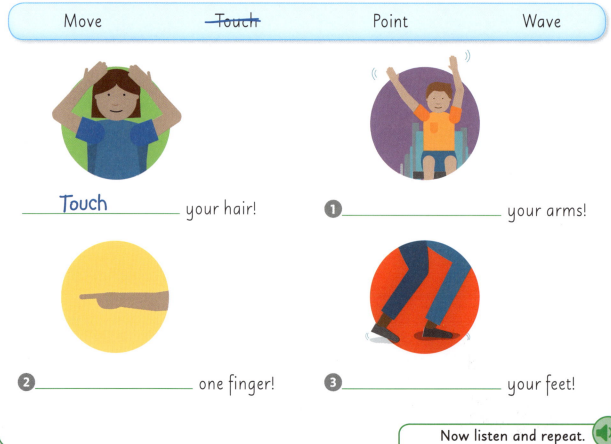

Touch your hair!　① _____ your arms!

② _____ one finger!　③ _____ your feet!

Now listen and repeat.

12 Our town

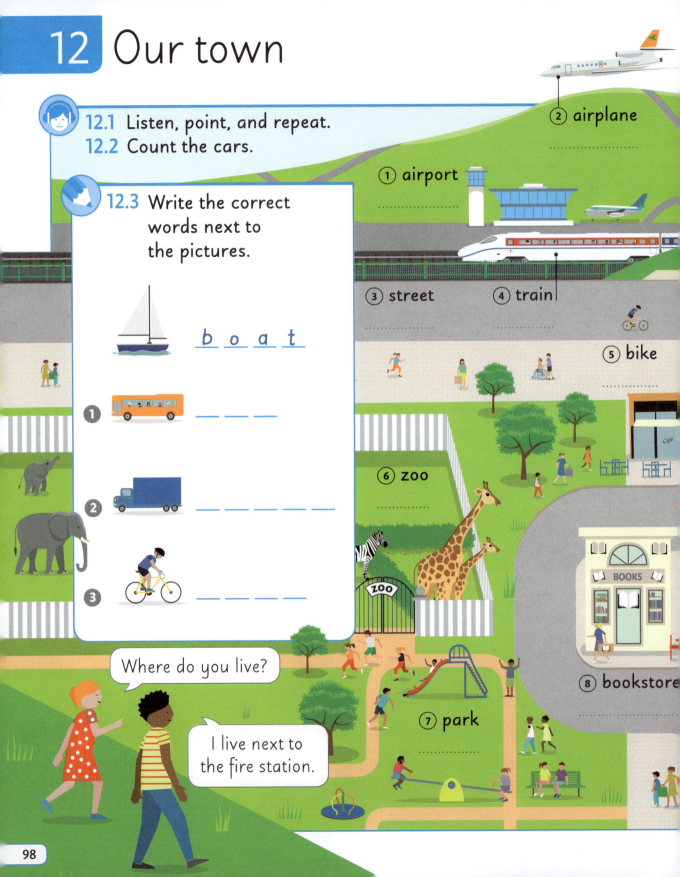

12.1 Listen, point, and repeat.
12.2 Count the cars.
12.3 Write the correct words next to the pictures.

b o a t

② airplane
① airport
③ street
④ train
⑤ bike
⑥ zoo
⑦ park
⑧ bookstore

Where do you live?
I live next to the fire station.

98

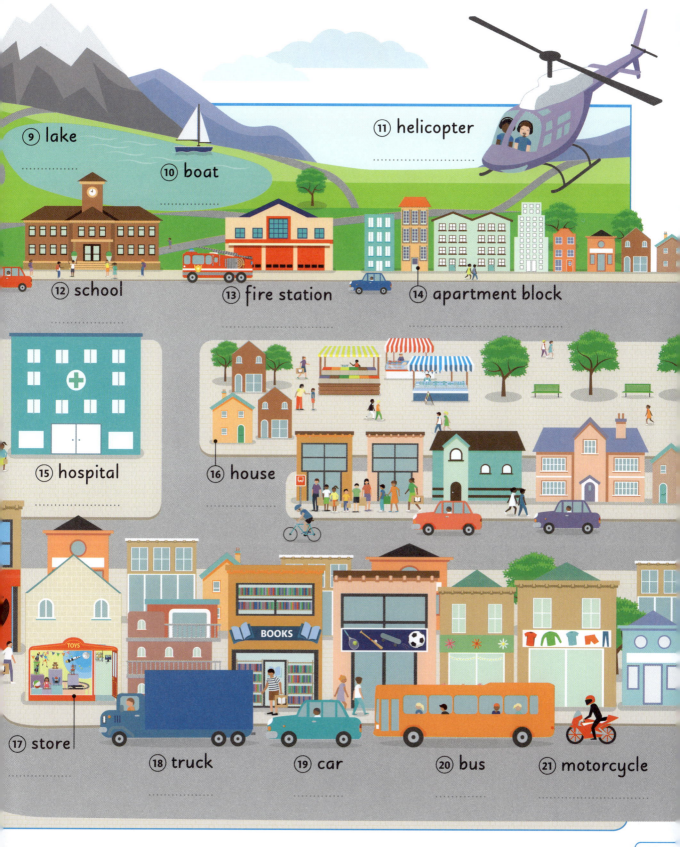

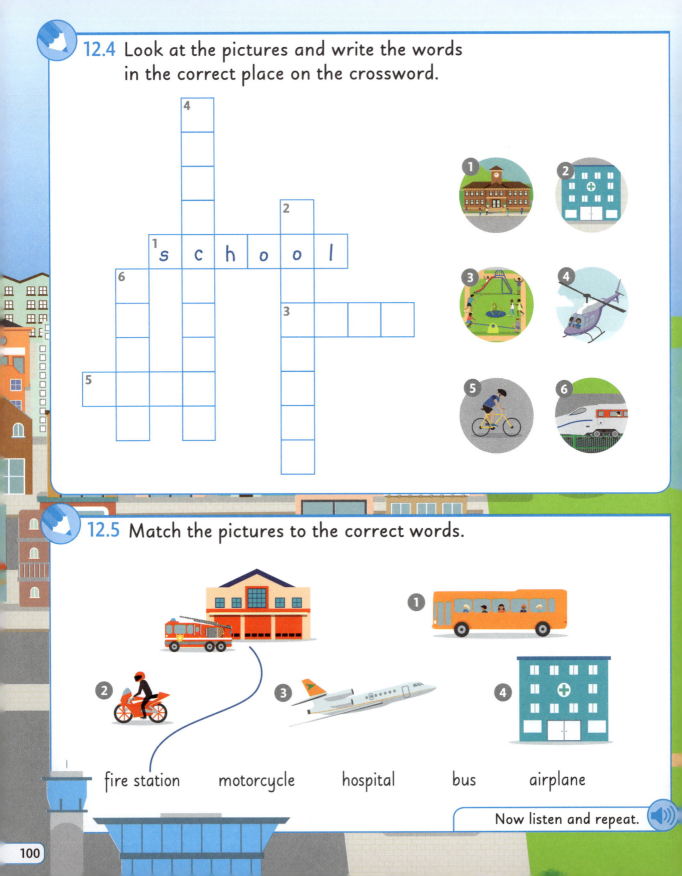

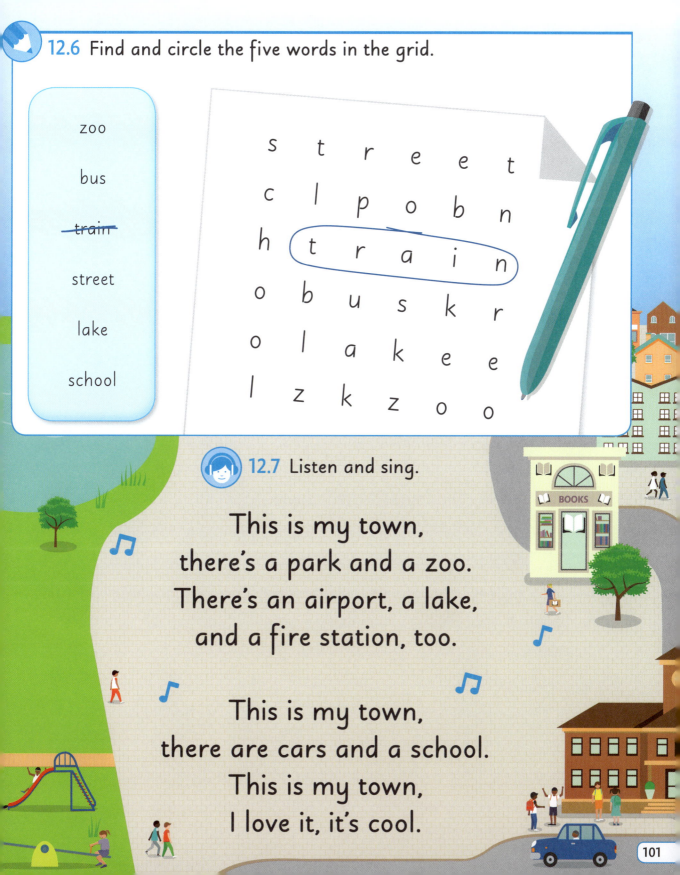

12.9 **Look at the pictures and circle the correct words.**

(There's) / There are a park.

❶ There's / There are two trucks.

❷ There's / There are a school.

❸ There's / There are a zoo.

❹ There's / There are four cars.

❺ There's / There are three boats.

Now listen and repeat.

12.10 Listen, point, and repeat.

① in front of ② behind ③ between ④ next to

12.11 Listen and read.

Where's my bike? It's in front of the store.

Where's my bike? It's behind the store.

Where's my bike?

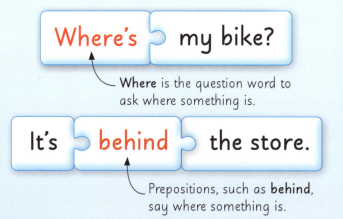

Where's — **my bike?**

Where is the question word to ask where something is.

It's — **behind** — **the store.**

Prepositions, such as **behind**, say where something is.

How it works

To ask about a thing's location, say **Where's**, followed by the thing. To describe where it is, say **It's**, then add a preposition and the location. Prepositions, such as **next to** or **behind**, describe the location of something.

Where is ➡ Where's

104

12.14 Listen and check off the correct pictures.

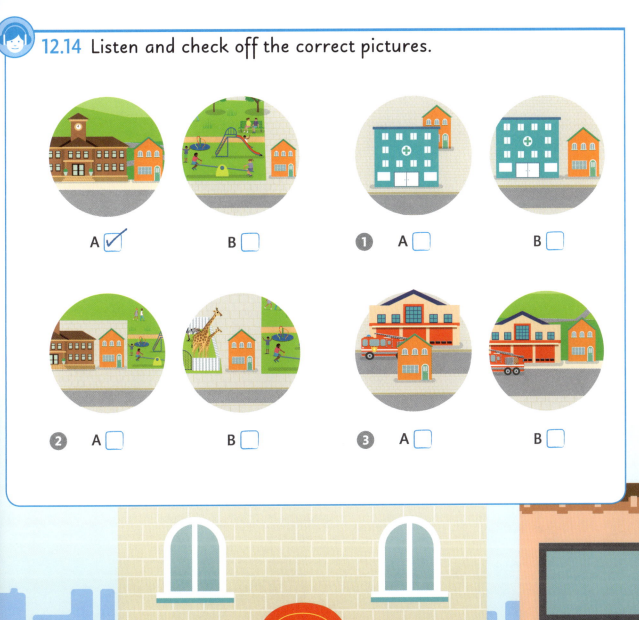

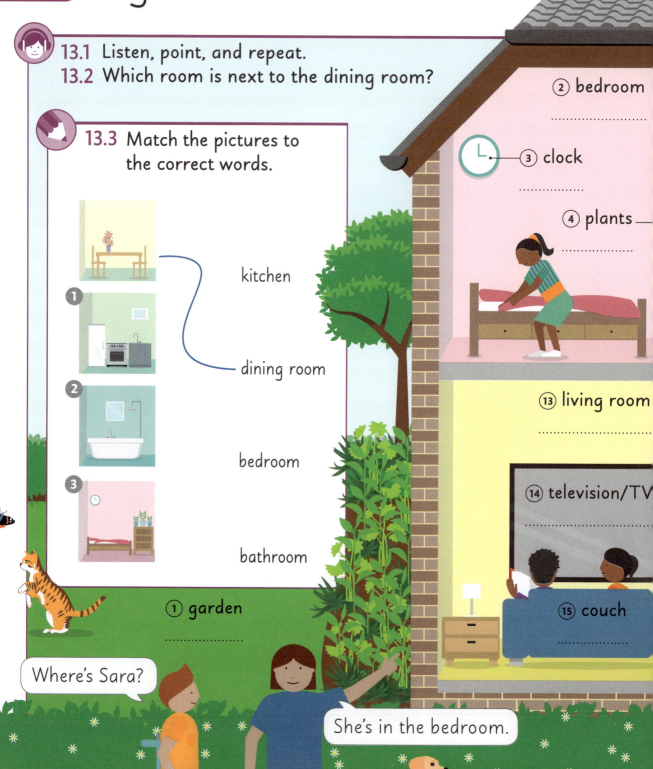

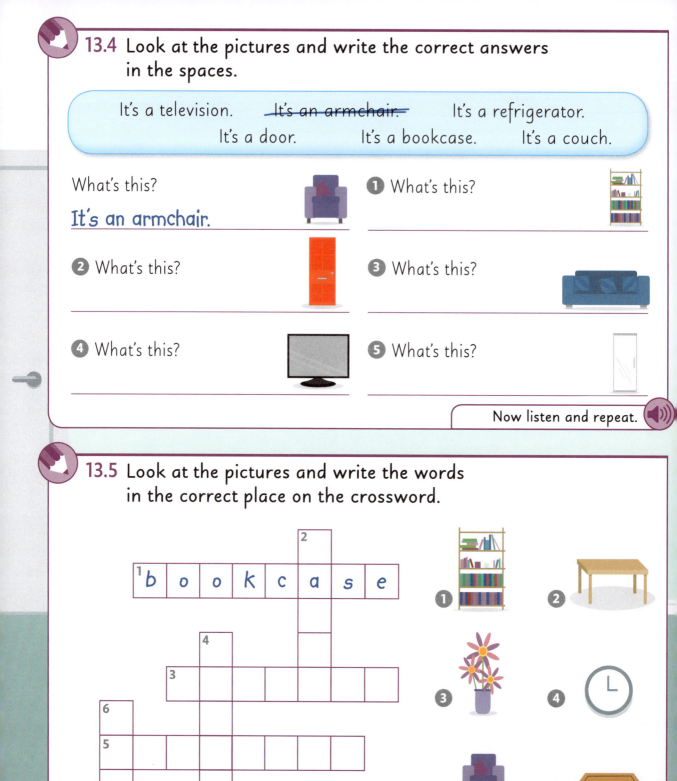

13.6 Look at the pictures and write the letters in the correct order.

t b e l a   h l l a

t a b l e   ❶ h _ _ _ _

p t l a n s   w n i w o d

❷ p _ _ _ _ _   ❸ w _ _ _ _ _

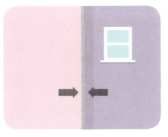

l g t s h i   w l a l

❹ l _ _ _ _ _   ❺ w _ _ _

Now listen and repeat.

111

13.7 Listen, point, and repeat.

① in   ② on   ③ under

13.8 Listen and read.

Where's the cat?

It's under the table!

Where's the cat?

Where's — the cat?

It's — under — the table.

This word describes where the cat is.

How it works
Use **Where's** to ask about someone or something's location. Prepositions, like **in**, **on**, and **under**, describe the thing or person's location.

Where is ➡ Where's

13.9 Listen and check off the correct pictures.

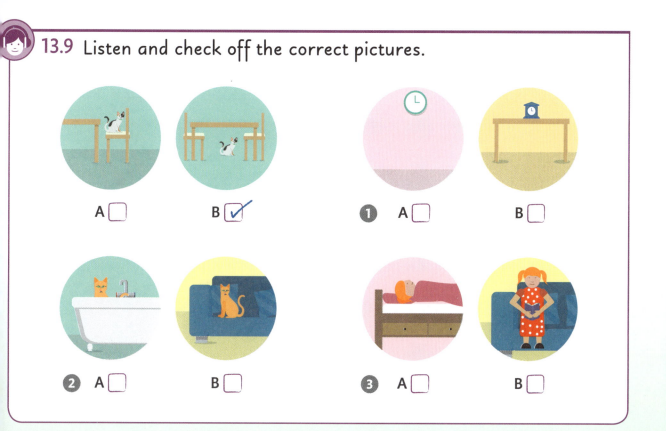

13.10 Listen and sing.

The TV's in the living room, the mat is in the hall.

Where's the clock? It's on my bedroom wall.

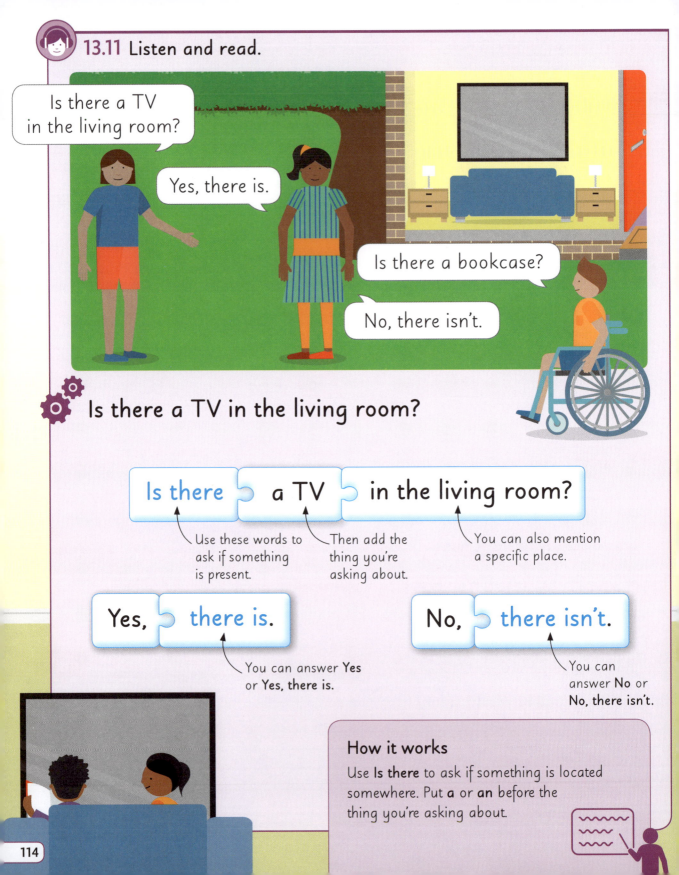

13.12 Look at the picture and write the correct answers in the spaces.

> Yes, there is. No, there isn't. ~~Yes, there is.~~
> No, there isn't. Yes, there is. No, there isn't.

Is there a TV in the living room?
Yes, there is.

❶ Is there a table in the kitchen?
_____

❷ Is there a clock in the kitchen?
_____

❸ Is there a bathtub in the bathroom?
_____

❹ Is there a couch in the living room?
_____

❺ Is there a bookcase in the bedroom?
_____

Now listen and repeat.

115

13.13 Listen and read.

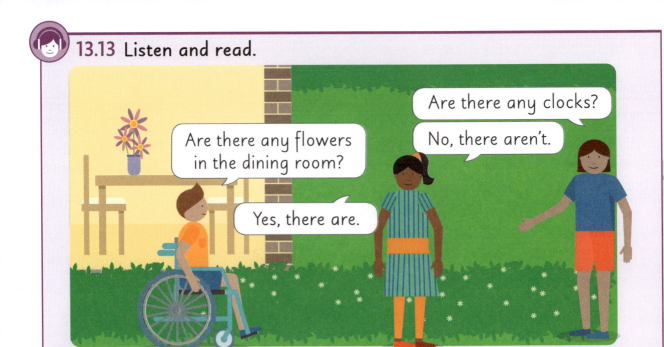

Are there any flowers in the dining room?

Are there any / flowers / in the dining room?

- Use these words to ask about two or more things.
- We use **any** after **Are there**.

Yes, there are.

No, there aren't.

- If the things are present, say **Yes** or **Yes, there are.**
- If the things aren't present, say **No** or **No, there aren't.**

How it works

Use **Are there** to ask if two or more things are located somewhere. When asking about two or more things, instead of **a** or **an**, use **any**, followed by the plural form of the thing you're asking about.

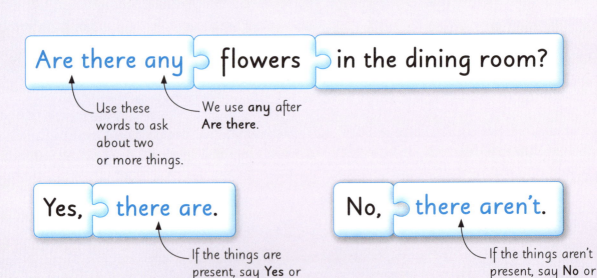

13.14 Look at the pictures and check off the correct answers.

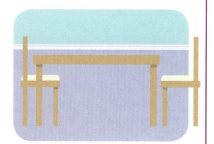

Are there any clocks?
Yes, there are. ☐
No, there aren't. ☑

① Are there any plants?
Yes, there are. ☐
No, there aren't. ☐

② Are there any chairs?
Yes, there are. ☐
No, there aren't. ☐

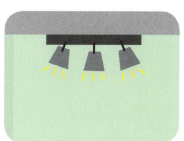

③ Are there any windows?
Yes, there are. ☐
No, there aren't. ☐

④ Are there any beds?
Yes, there are. ☐
No, there aren't. ☐

⑤ Are there any lights?
Yes, there are. ☐
No, there aren't. ☐

Now listen and repeat.

14 Review: Where I live

 14.1 Listen and read.

I'm Maria and this is my home. I live next to a park.

In my home, there's a dining room and a kitchen. There are two bedrooms. That is my bedroom. There's a clock and a toy box in my bedroom. My favorite toy is my teddy bear.

14.2 Write about your home and draw your bedroom.

I'm _____ and this is my home.
I live _____.

In my home, there's a _____ and a _____. There are _____.
That is my bedroom. There's a _____ and a _____ in my bedroom.
My favorite toy is my _____.

15 On the farm

15.1 Listen, point, and repeat.
15.2 Count the sheep.

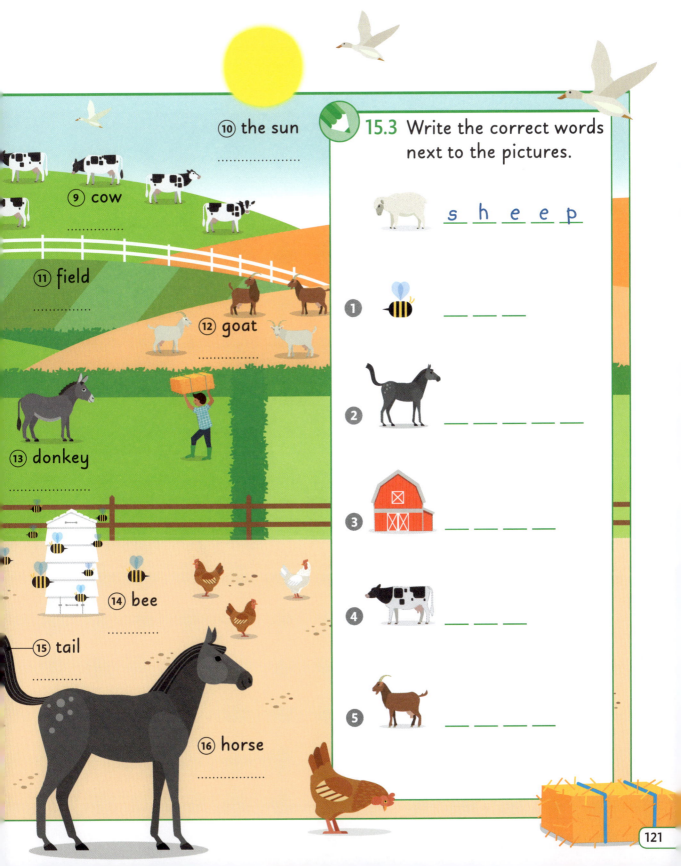

15.4 Match the pictures to the correct words.

- tractor
- chicken
- barn
- tail
- donkey
- the sun

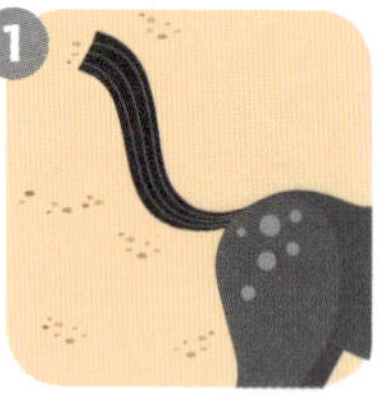

Now listen and repeat.

15.5 Look at the pictures and write the letters in the correct order.

s p e h e
s h e e p

1. g t o a
   g _ _ _

2. h e r s o
   h _ _ _ _

3. d k c u
   d _ _ _

4. t e r e
   t _ _ _

Now listen and repeat.

15.6 Look at the pictures and write the words in the correct place on the crossword.

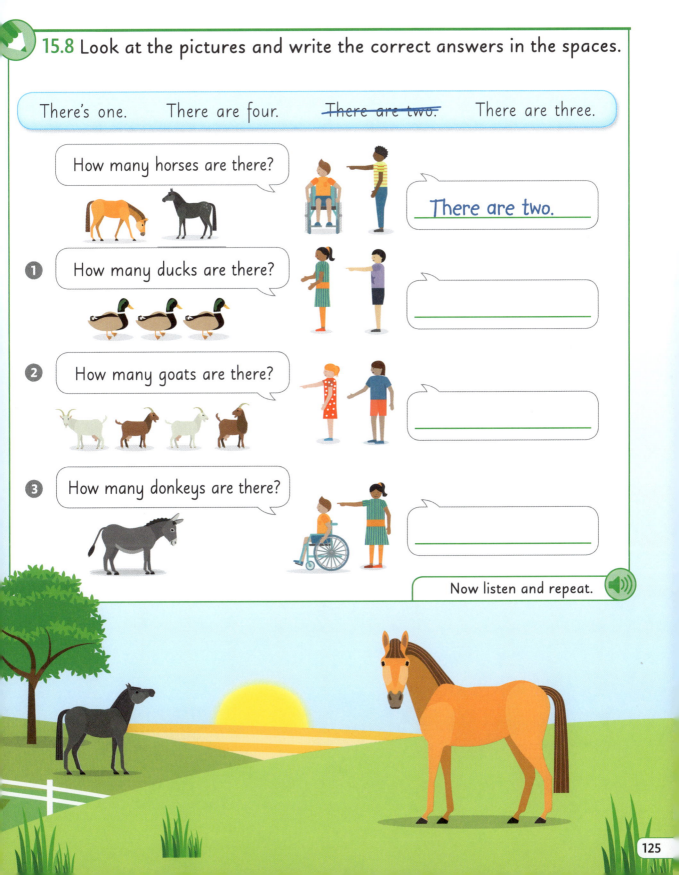

15.10 Listen and match the questions to the correct answers.

Where are the ducks?   They're in front of the barn.
1. Where are the horses?   They're in the field.
2. Where are the chickens?   They're in the barn.
3. Where are the goats?   They're in the pond.
4. Where are the donkeys?   They're next to the pond.
5. Where are the pigs?   They're under the tree.

15.11 Listen and sing.

Where are the ducks?
They're in the pond!

Where are the goats?
They're in the field!

Where are the cows?
They're in the barn!

Where are the animals?
They're on my farm!

127

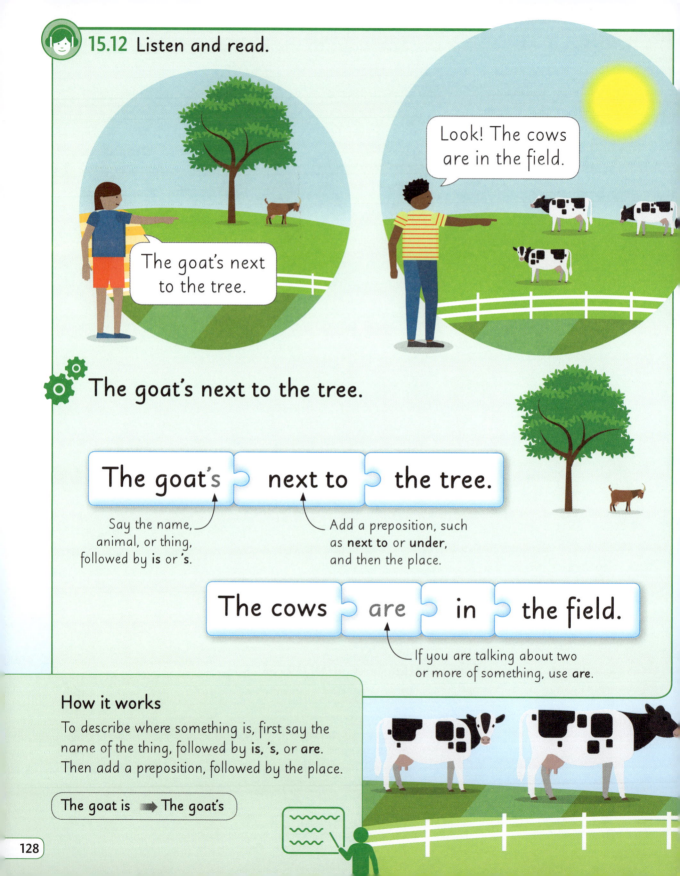

15.13 Read the story. Then look at the picture and write the correct words in the spaces.

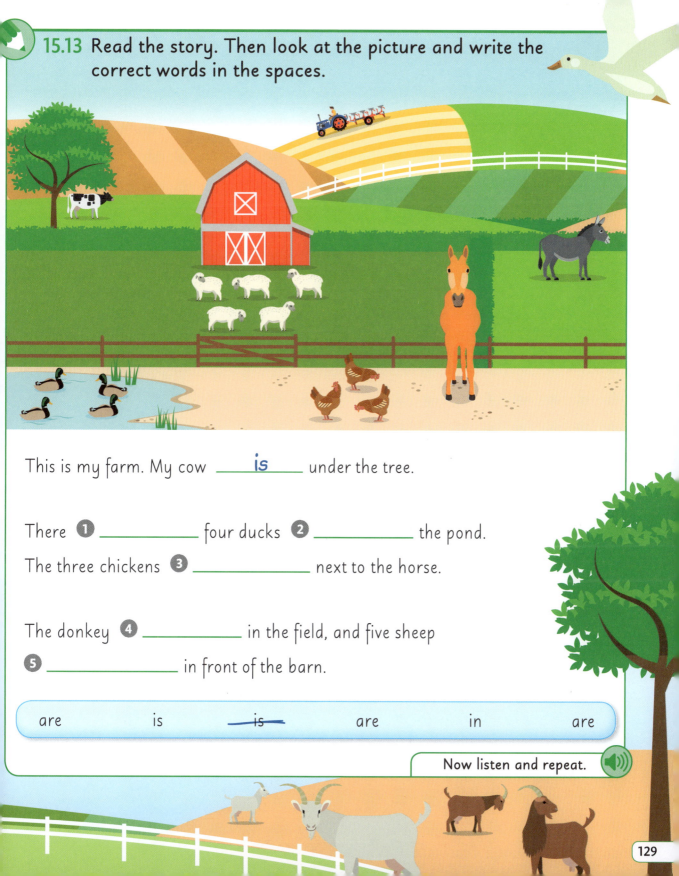

This is my farm. My cow ____is____ under the tree.

There ❶ _____ four ducks ❷ _____ the pond.
The three chickens ❸ _____ next to the horse.

The donkey ❹ _____ in the field, and five sheep
❺ _____ in front of the barn.

| are | is | ~~is~~ | are | in | are |

Now listen and repeat.

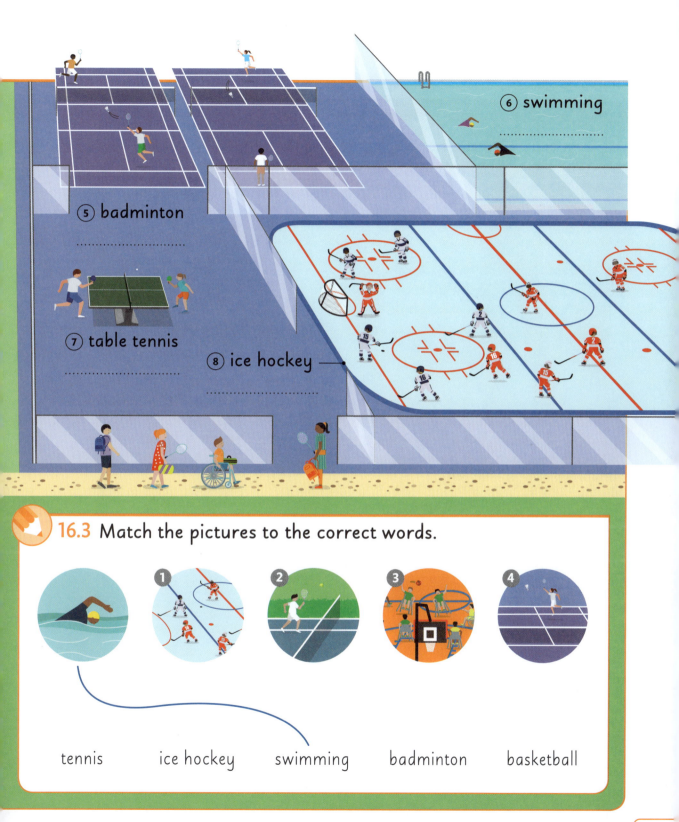

⑤ badminton
⑥ swimming
⑦ table tennis
⑧ ice hockey

16.3 Match the pictures to the correct words.

tennis   ice hockey   swimming   badminton   basketball

16.4 Look at the pictures and check off the correct words.

badminton ☐
ice hockey ✓
tennis ☐

table tennis ☐
badminton ☐
swimming ☐

baseball ☐
soccer ☐
basketball ☐

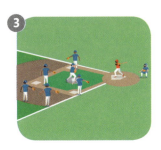

tennis ☐
baseball ☐
swimming ☐

Now listen and repeat.

16.5 Look at the pictures and circle the correct words.

(basketball) / swimming　❶ tennis / ice hockey　❷ badminton / baseball

❸ soccer / swimming　❹ table tennis / soccer

Now listen and repeat.

 16.6 Listen, point, and repeat.

① run

② jump

③ swim

④ play tennis

⑤ play ice hockey

⑥ catch

⑦ bounce

⑧ kick

⑨ throw

 ⑩ hit

16.7 Listen and check off the correct pictures.

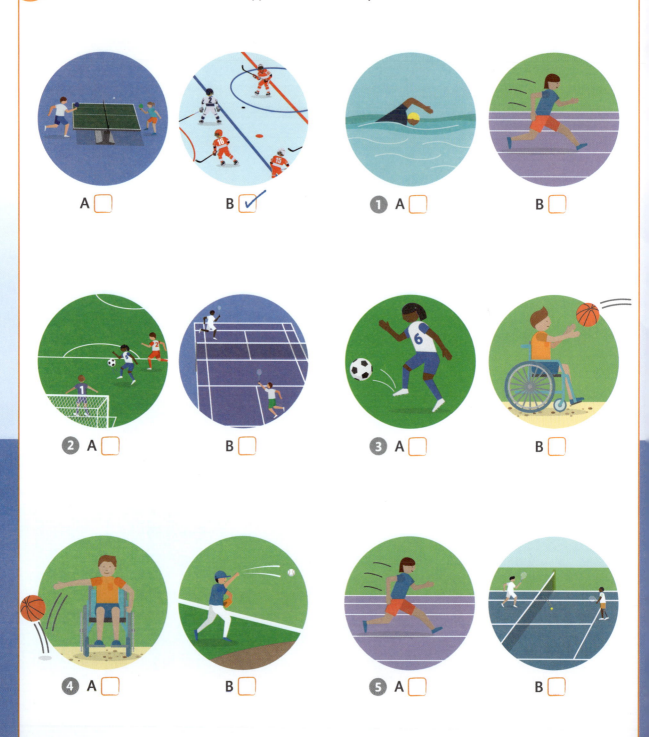

16.8 Look at the pictures and write the letters in the correct order.

j p m u   c c h t a   s m i w

j u m p   ① c _ _ _ _ _   ② s _ _ _ _

t o w r h   k k c i   b c n o u e

③ t _ _ _ _ _   ④ k _ _ _ _   ⑤ b _ _ _ _ _ _

Now listen and repeat.

16.9 Listen and read.

I can play basketball.

| I | can | play basketball. | I | can't | play baseball. |

Use **can** if you are able to do something.

Use **can't** if you are unable to do something.

How it works
Can is a modal verb used to talk about things you are able to do. The negative form is **can't**.

Cannot ➡ Can't

136

16.10 Listen and check off the correct sentences.

I can play baseball. ☐
I can't play baseball. ☑

1

I can catch a ball. ☐
I can't catch a ball. ☐

2

I can play ice hockey. ☐
I can't play ice hockey. ☐

3

I can hit a ball. ☐
I can't hit a ball. ☐

4

I can swim. ☐
I can't swim. ☐

5

I can play table tennis. ☐
I can't play table tennis. ☐

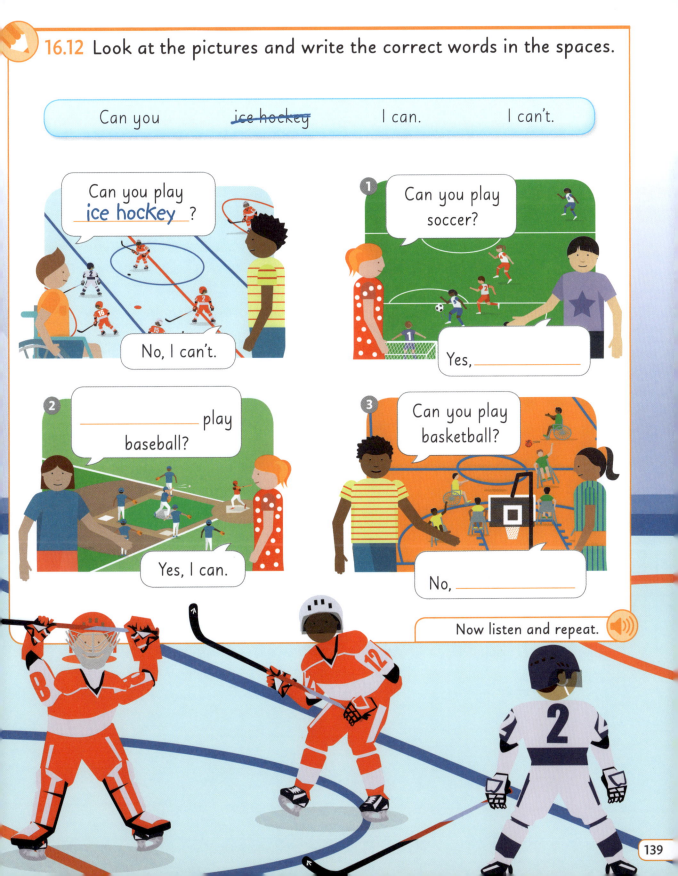

16.14 **Listen and write the correct answers in the spaces.**

> No, she can't.   ~~No, he can't.~~
>   Yes, she can.   Yes, he can.

Can Andy play tennis?   No, he can't.

① Can Sara play badminton?

② Can Sofia play ice hockey?

③ Can Max play table tennis?

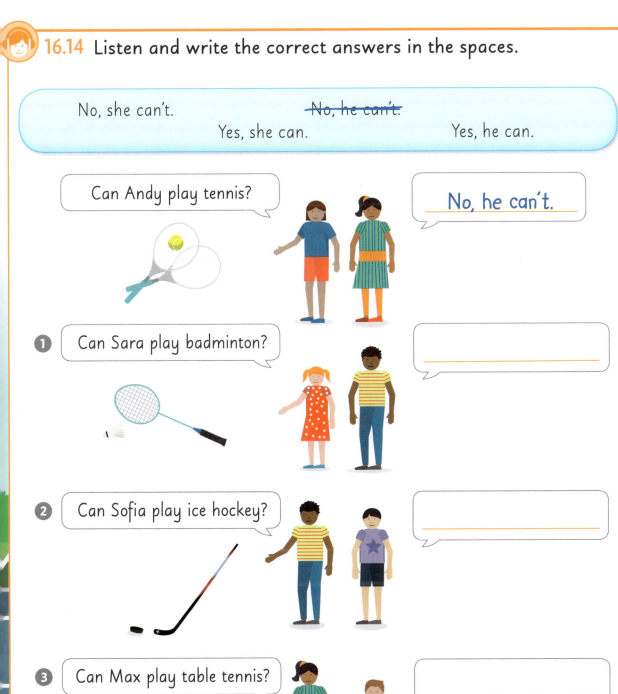

17 At the food market

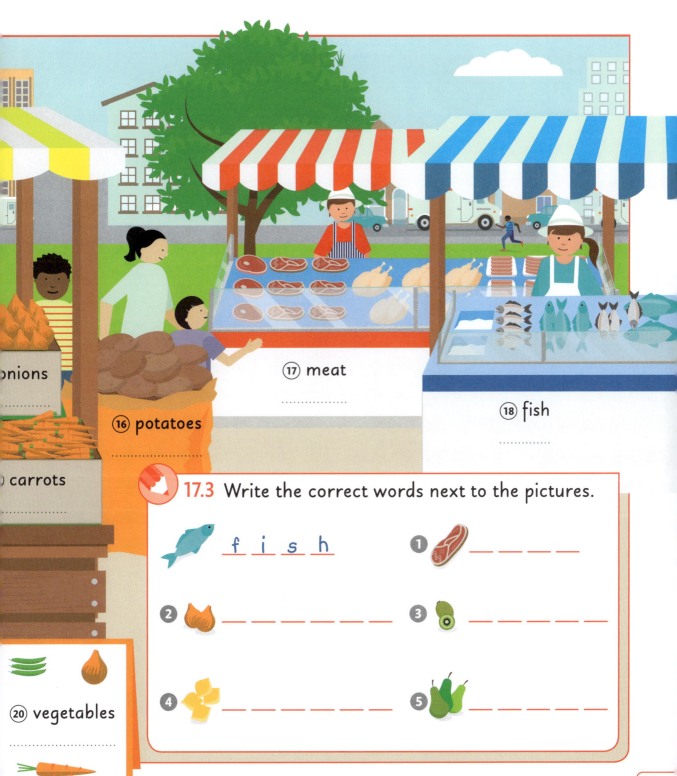

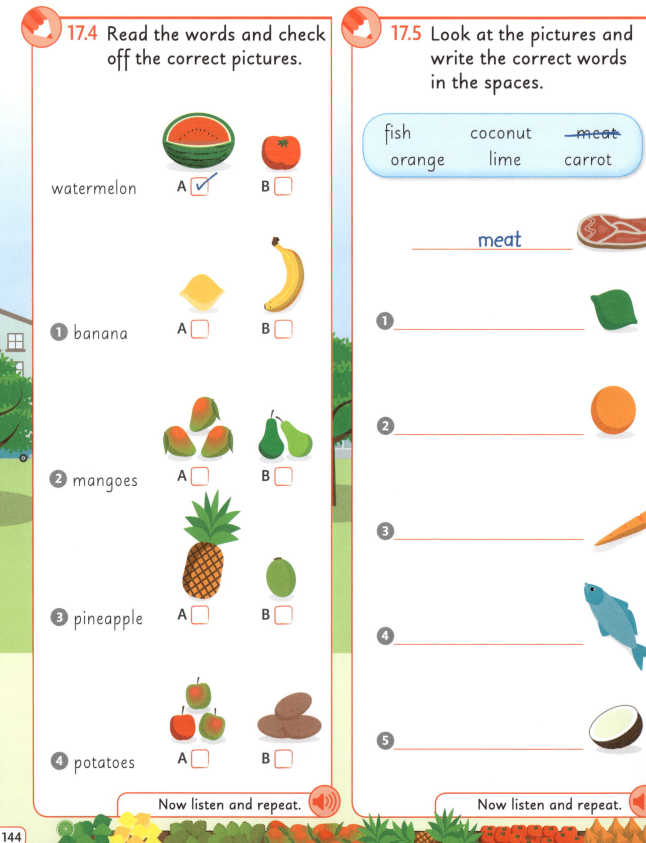

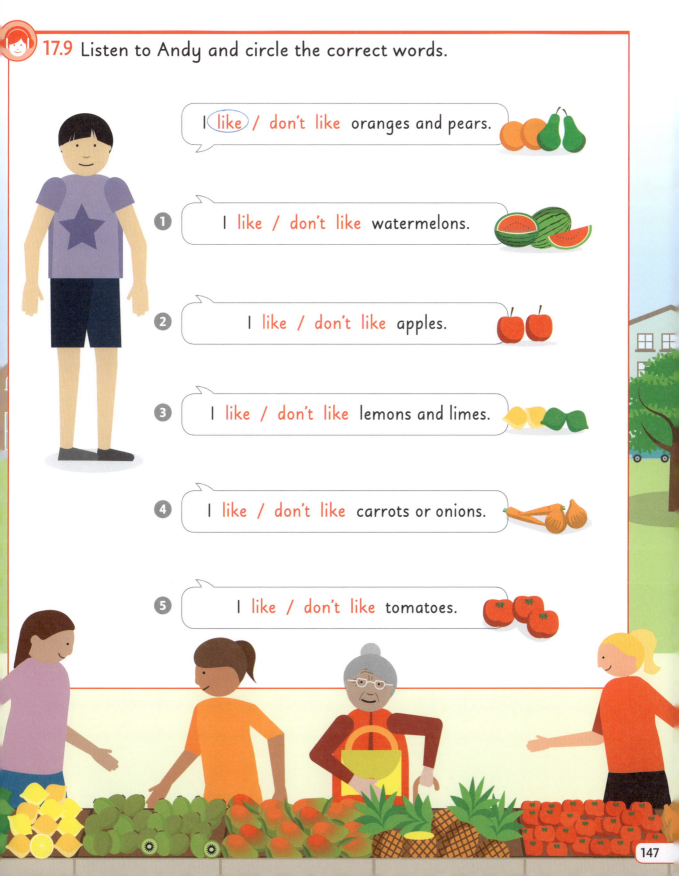

17.10 Listen and read.

Do you like apples?

Say this to ask someone if they like something.

You can answer **Yes** or **Yes, I do.**

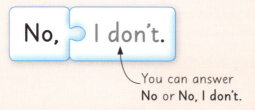

You can answer **No** or **No, I don't.**

How it works

To ask someone a question in the **present simple**, put **Do you** before the verb.

Some words form the plural differently from most nouns. If the name of the fruit or vegetable ends with an **o**, add **es** to the singular form rather than just **s**.

Tomato	➡	Tomatoes
Potato	➡	Potatoes
Mango	➡	Mangoes

17.11 Look at the pictures and write the correct words in the spaces.

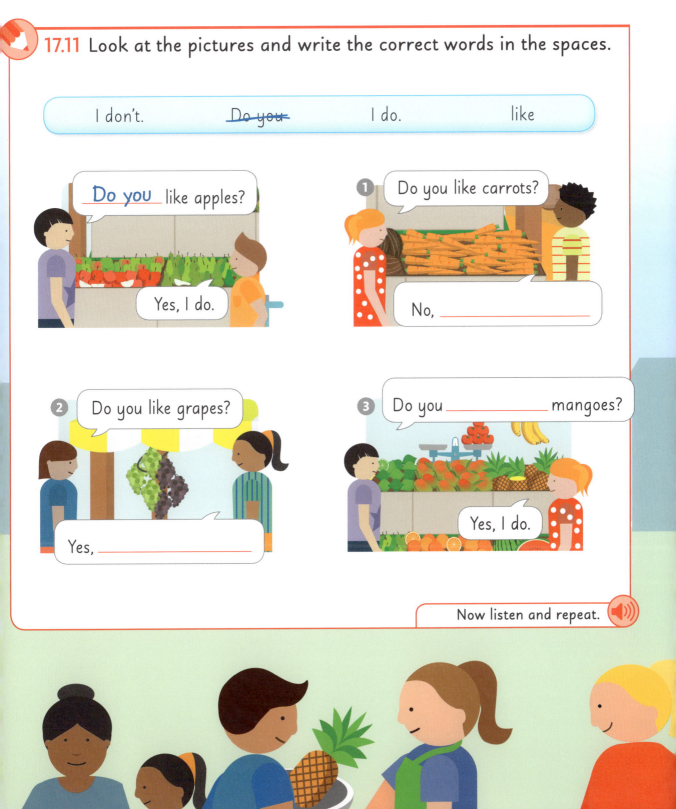

Now listen and repeat.

17.13 Look at the pictures and write the correct words in the spaces.

an   ~~some~~   a   some

May I have _____some_____ kiwis, please?

❶ May I have _____ banana, please?

❷ May I have _____ orange, please?

❸ May I have _____ vegetables, please?

Now listen and repeat.

18 At the toy store

18.1 Listen, point, and repeat.
18.2 How many stars are there?

18.3 Match the pictures to the correct words.

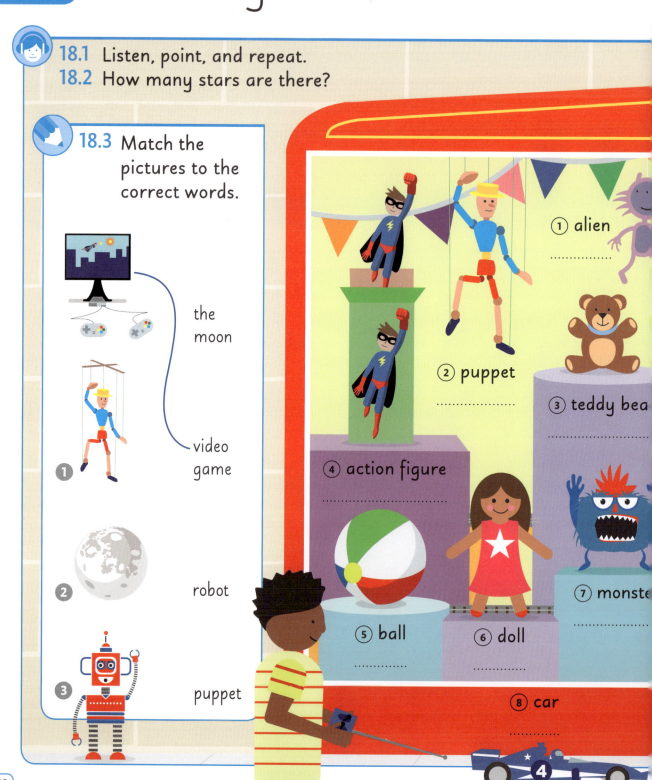

1 — the moon / video game
2 — robot
3 — puppet

① alien
② puppet
③ teddy bear
④ action figure
⑤ ball
⑥ doll
⑦ monster
⑧ car

18.4 Look at the pictures and check off the correct words.

teddy bear ✓
robot ☐
train ☐

1   board game ☐
monster ☐
video game ☐

2   the moon ☐
puppet ☐
car ☐

3   action figure ☐
ball ☐
rocket ☐

Now listen and repeat. 🔊

18.5 Write the correct words next to the pictures.

rocket   ~~the moon~~   alien   robot

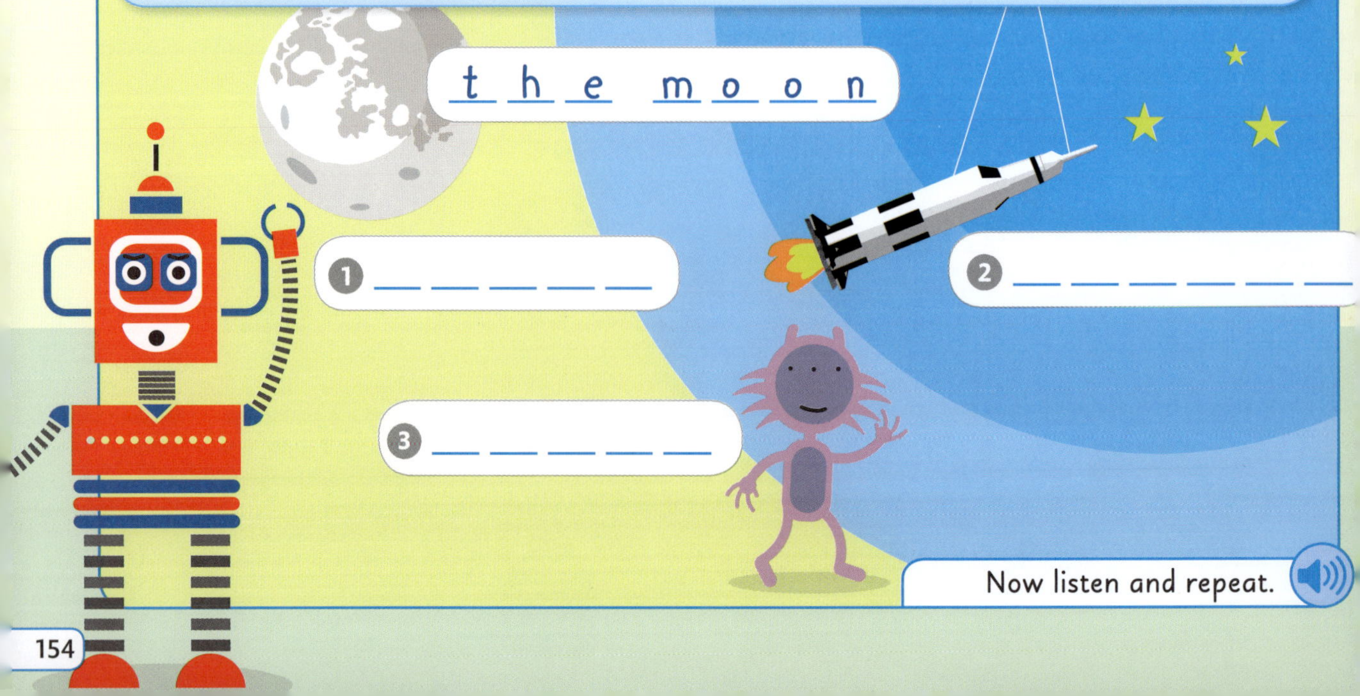

t h e   m o o n

1 _ _ _ _ _ _ _ _

2 _ _ _ _ _ _ _ _

3 _ _ _ _ _ _ _ _

Now listen and repeat. 🔊

154

18.8 **Look at the pictures and write the correct words in the spaces.**

rockets   ~~cars~~   trains   video games

Sofia likes _____cars_____ . Her cousin Eva doesn't like

❶ _____ . Ben likes ❷ _____ , but

his friend Sam doesn't like ❸ _____ .

Now listen and read.

18.9 **Listen and write the correct words in the spaces.**

likes   doesn't like   ~~likes~~   doesn't like

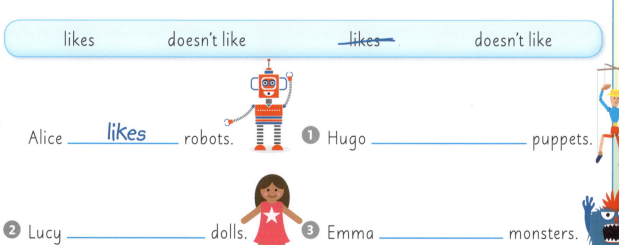

Alice ___likes___ robots.   ❶ Hugo _____ puppets.

❷ Lucy _____ dolls.   ❸ Emma _____ monsters.

18.10 Listen and read.

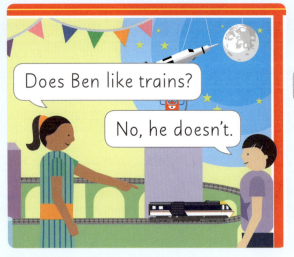

Does he like trains?

Does he **like** **trains?**

To form a question, put **Does** before **he**, **she**, or someone's name.

Then add **like**. Don't add an **s** to the verb when you use it in a question.

Yes, **he does.**   **No,** **he doesn't.**

Answer **Yes** or Yes, he does.

Answer **No** or No, he doesn't.

How it works

To ask a question with **he** or **she**, start the question with **Does**, not **Do**. Do not add an **s** to **like**.

158

18.11 Listen and check off the correct answers.

Does he like robots?

Yes, he does. ✓
No, he doesn't. ☐

1 Does she like dolls?

Yes, she does. ☐
No, she doesn't. ☐

2 Does he like video games?

Yes, he does. ☐
No, he doesn't. ☐

3 Does she like monsters?

Yes, she does. ☐
No, she doesn't. ☐

4 Does he like action figures?

Yes, he does. ☐
No, he doesn't. ☐

5 Does she like balloons?

Yes, she does. ☐
No, she doesn't. ☐

18.12 There are four sentences. Mark the beginning and end of each one and write them below.

Doesheliketrains?No,hedoesn't.Doesshelikedolls?Yes,shedoes.

Does he like trains?

1 _____

2 _____

3 _____

Now listen and repeat.

159

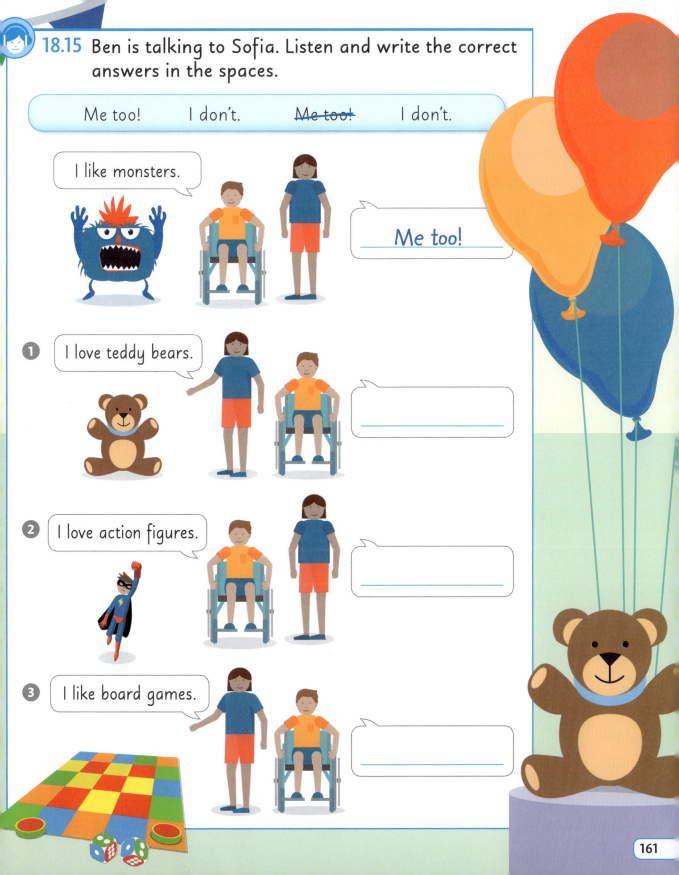

19 Our hobbies

19.1 Listen, point, and repeat.
19.2 Where is Sofia?

19.3 Match the pictures to the correct words.

dance

read

draw pictures

take photos

sing

① ride a bike
② watch soccer
③ skateboard
④ draw pictures
⑤ paint

I enjoy painting.

Me too. It's fun!

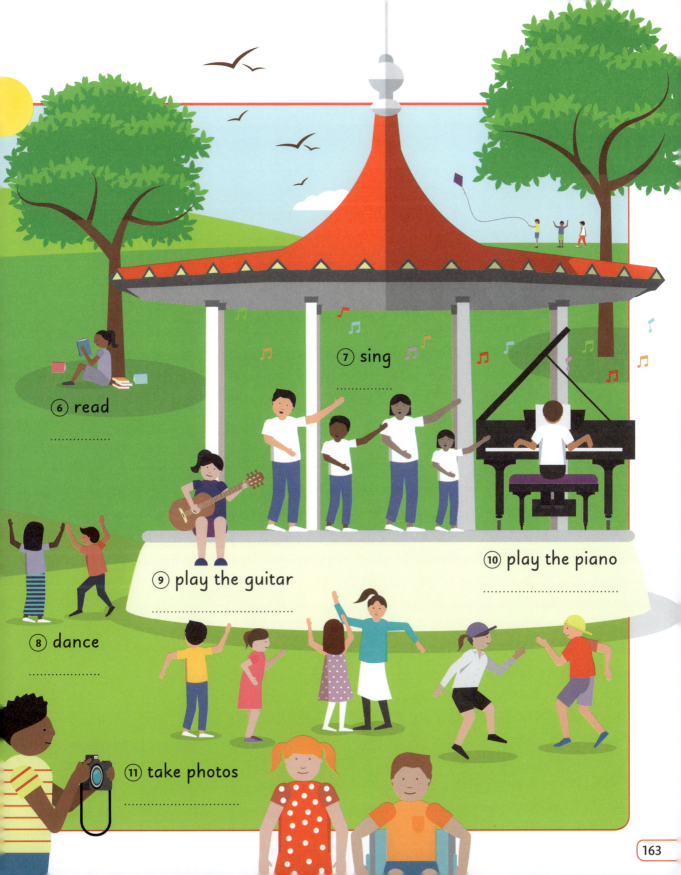

19.4 Listen and check off the correct pictures.

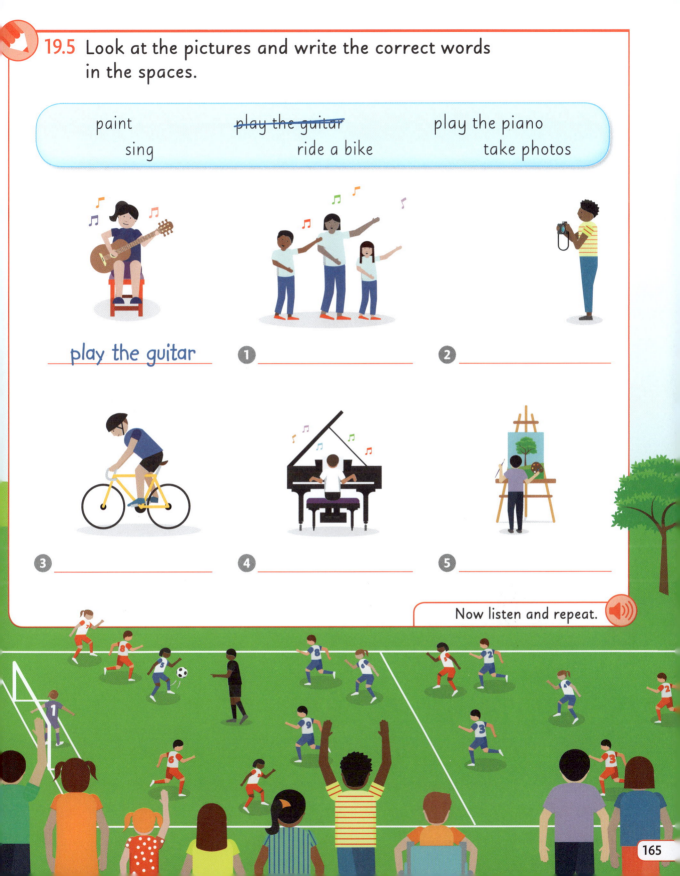

19.7 Listen and match the names to the correct pictures.

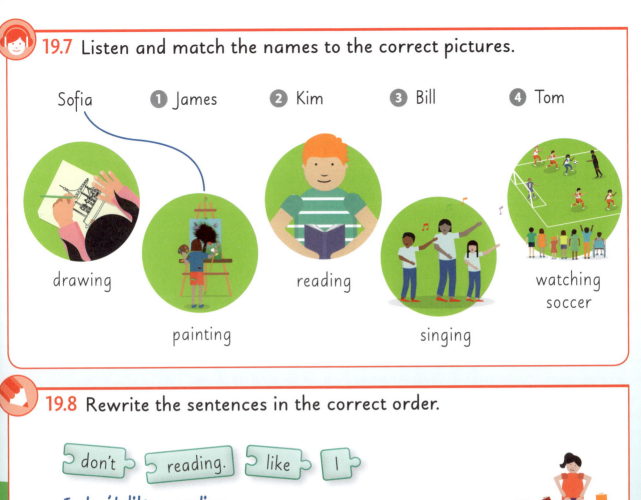

19.8 Rewrite the sentences in the correct order.

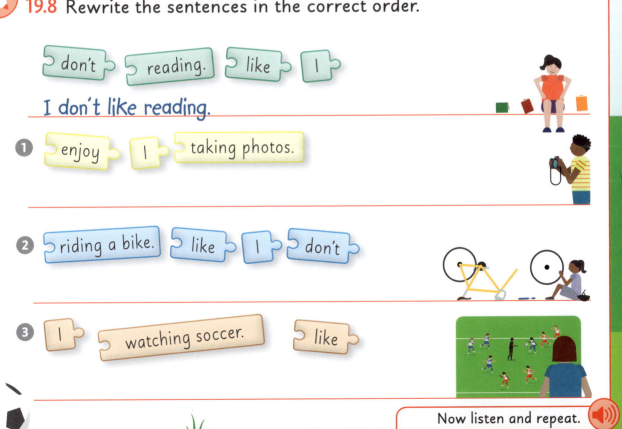

I don't like reading.

19.10 Andy and Sofia are talking. Listen and check off the correct answers.

Do you like singing?
Yes, I do. ✓
No, I don't. ☐

1 Do you like playing the guitar?
Yes, I do. ☐
No, I don't. ☐

2 Do you like dancing?
Yes, I do. ☐
No, I don't. ☐

3 Do you like painting?
Yes, I do. ☐
No, I don't. ☐

4 Do you like riding a bike?
Yes, I do. ☐
No, I don't. ☐

19.11 Listen and sing.

Do you have hobbies?
Yes, I do.
I love reading books
and skateboarding, too.

Do you like playing tennis?
Yes, I do.
I love playing tennis
and playing soccer, too.

Do you enjoy singing?
Yes, I do.
I love singing songs,
and I love dancing, too.

20 Review: What I like

 20.1 Listen and read.

My name's Sofia. I like skateboarding and trains. I don't like painting. I can play tennis and swim. I can't play the piano. I like mangoes, but I don't like apples.

My friend Max likes cars. He doesn't like board games. He likes oranges, but he doesn't like bananas.

20.2 Write about the things you and a friend like and draw a picture.

My name's _____
I like _____ and _____.
I don't like _____. I can _____
and _____. I can't _____.
I like _____, but I don't like _____.
My friend likes _____.
My friend doesn't like _____.

21 Our party clothes

21.1 Listen, point, and repeat.
21.2 What color is Sara's jacket?

1. watch
2. sock
3. skirt
4. shorts
5. pants
6. T-shirt
7. hat
8. dress
9. purse

Happy birthday, Ben!

Thank you, Maria!

172

21.3 Write the correct words next to the pictures.

s h i r t

1. _ _ _

2. _ _ _ _ _ _ _

3. _ _ _

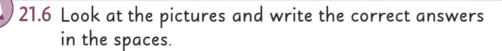

21.6 Look at the pictures and write the correct answers in the spaces.

> It's a watch.　　　It's a sock.　　~~It's a skirt.~~
> 　　It's a T-shirt.　　It's a jacket.　　It's a shoe.

What's this?

It's a skirt.

① What's this?

_____

② What's this?

_____

③ What's this?

_____

④ What's this?

_____

⑤ What's this?

_____

Now listen and repeat.

21.7 Listen and sing.

We're at a party,
so let's all dance and play.
What a fun party
for Ben's birthday!

Andy's wearing his
favorite T-shirt,
and Sara has
a beautiful skirt.

175

21.9 Listen and check off the correct pictures.

21.11 Look at the pictures and check off the correct answers.

Are you wearing my hat?

Yes, I am. ☐
No, I'm not. ☑

① Are you wearing my jacket?

Yes, I am. ☐
No, I'm not. ☐

② Are you wearing my watch?

Yes, I am. ☐
No, I'm not. ☐

③ Are you wearing my glasses?

Yes, I am. ☐
No, I'm not. ☐

Now listen and repeat.

21.13 Look at the pictures and write the correct words in the spaces.

> What a   ~~What a~~   What a   What a
> What a   What   What

___What a___ clean T-shirt!

1. _____ beautiful boots!

2. _____ dirty sock!

3. _____ nice glasses!

4. _____ nice shirt!

5. _____ big purse!

Now listen and repeat.

22 Our day at the beach

22.1 Listen, point, and repeat.
22.2 How many balls are there?

1. seagull
2. ship
3. surf
4. jellyfish
5. fly a kite
6. sand
7. play soccer
8. bucket
9. shovel
10. listen to music
11. drink juice
12. eat ice cream

Maria's eating ice cream.

Sofia's drinking juice.

182

⑬ fish

swim in the ocean

⑮ run on the beach

⑯ read a book

⑰ throw a ball

⑱ shell

22.3 Match the pictures to the correct words.

play soccer

1 — surf

2 drink juice

3 listen to music

4 read a book

5 throw a ball

183

22.4 **Look at the pictures and write the correct answers in the spaces.**

> It's a seagull.   ~~It's a jellyfish.~~   It's a shovel.
> It's a shell.   It's a ship.   It's a bucket.

What's this?
It's a jellyfish.

① What's this?
_____

② What's this?
_____

③ What's this?
_____

④ What's this?
_____

⑤ What's this?
_____

Now listen and repeat.

22.5 **Listen and check off the correct pictures.**

A ☐   B ✓   ① A ☐   B ☐   ② A ☐   B ☐

③ A ☐   B ☐   ④ A ☐   B ☐   ⑤ A ☐   B ☐

184

22.6 Look at the pictures and write the letters in the correct order.

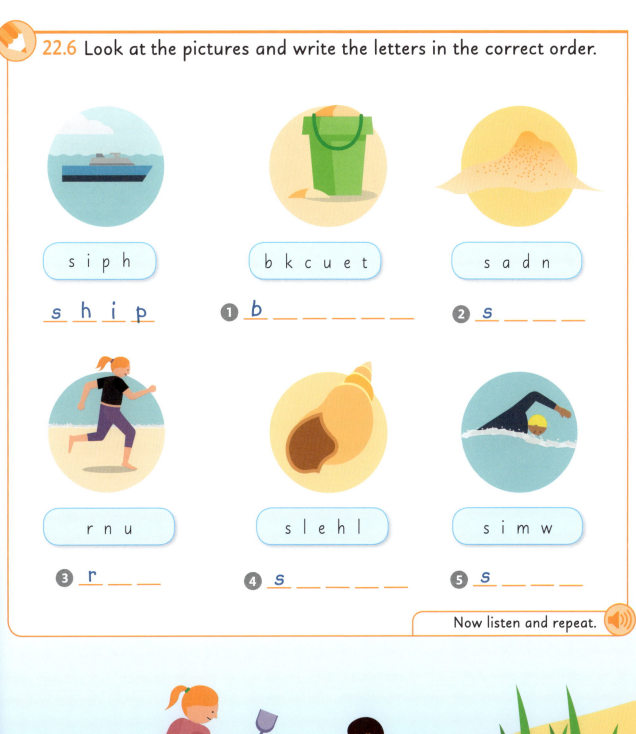

s i p h
<u>s</u> <u>h</u> <u>i</u> <u>p</u>

b k c u e t
① <u>b</u> _ _ _ _ _

s a d n
② <u>s</u> _ _ _

r n u
③ <u>r</u> _ _

s l e h l
④ <u>s</u> _ _ _ _

s i m w
⑤ <u>s</u> _ _ _

Now listen and repeat.

22.8 Look at the pictures and check off the correct answers.

He's listening to music. ✓
He isn't listening to music. ☐

① She's swimming. ☐
She isn't swimming. ☐

② He's flying a kite. ☐
He isn't flying a kite. ☐

③ She's drinking juice. ☐
She isn't drinking juice. ☐

Now listen and repeat.

22.9 Listen and match the names to the correct pictures.

Nick ① May ② Pat ③ Mark ④ Lucy

swimming   throwing a ball   fishing   playing soccer   flying a kite

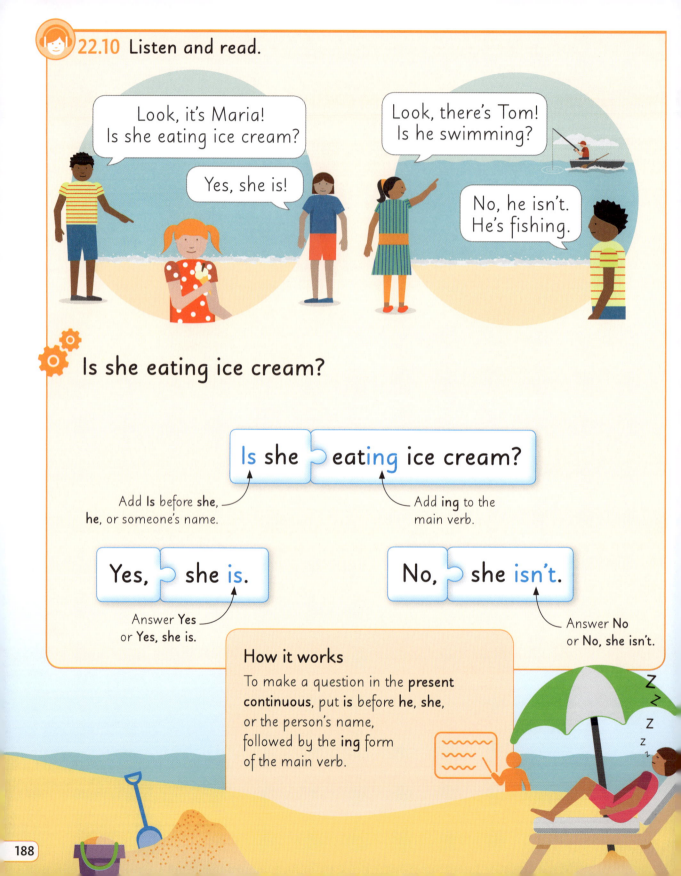

22.11 Look at the pictures and write the correct answers in the spaces.

Yes, he is.   ~~No, he isn't.~~   Yes, she is.   No, she isn't.

Is Tom swimming?
No, he isn't.

1 Is she fishing?

2 Is Sue surfing?

3 Is he running?

Now listen and repeat.

189

23 Lunchtime

23.1 Listen, point, and repeat.
23.2 What is Sofia eating?

23.3 Write the correct words under the pictures.

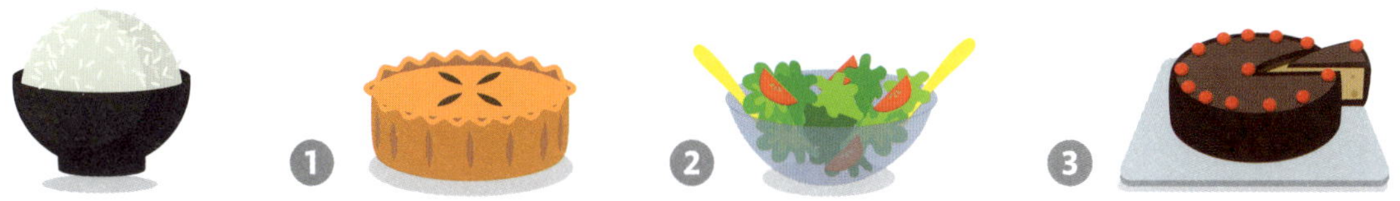

r i c e　　 _ _ _　　 _ _ _ _ _　　 _ _ _ _

⑩ chocolate

⑪ noodles

⑫ drinks

⑬ fruit

⑭ juice

⑮ water

⑯ lemonade

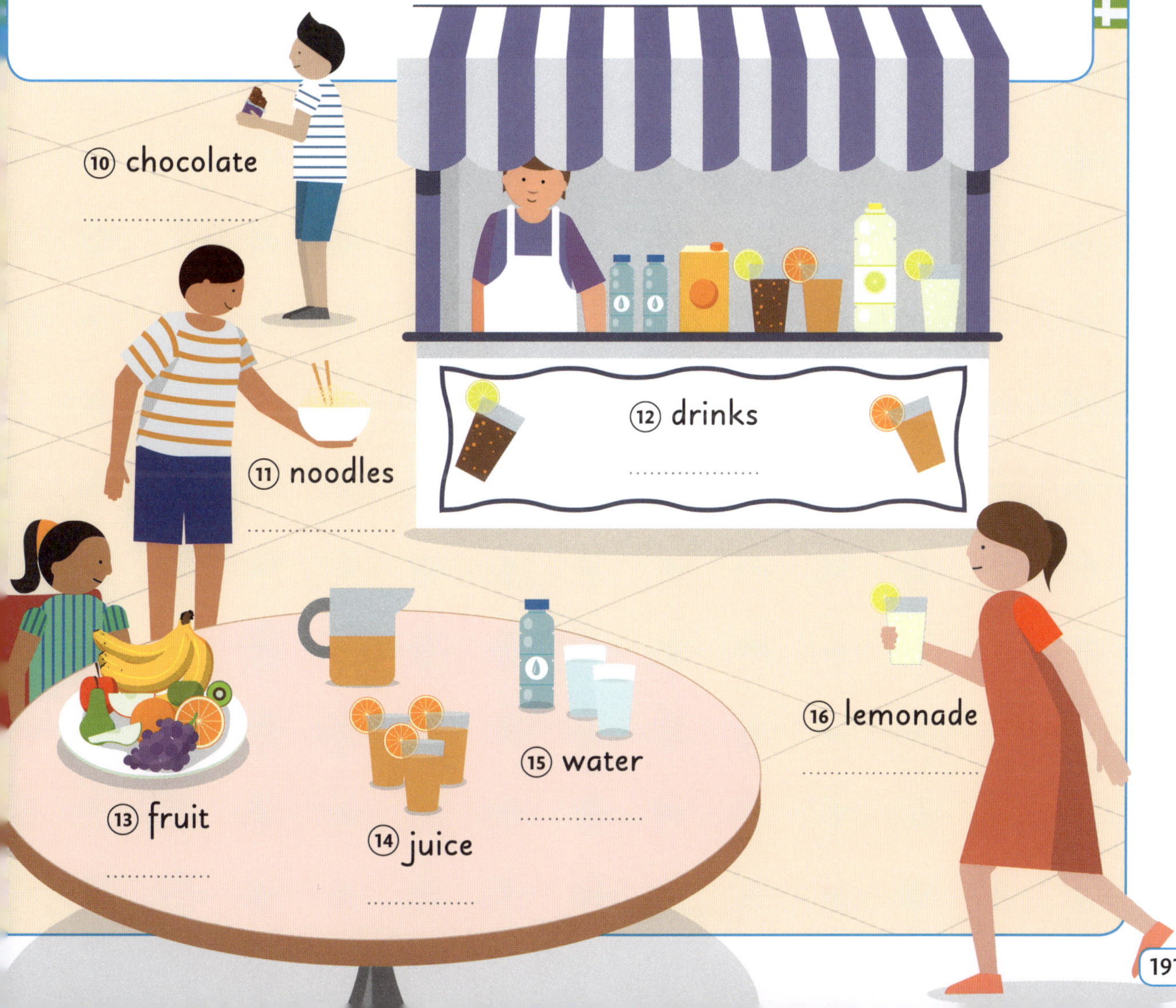

23.4 Look at the pictures and circle the correct words.

sausages / (pie)

1
cake / orange

2
chocolate / fruit

3
juice / noodles

4
rice / candy

5
burger / salad

Now listen and repeat.

23.5 Listen and check off the correct pictures.

A ☐   B ✓

1
A ☐   B ☐

2
A ☐   B ☐

3
A ☐   B ☐

23.6 Look at the pictures and write the correct words in the spaces.

fruit ~~water~~ burger sausages fries lemonade

water

1. _____
2. _____ 
3. _____ 
4. _____ 
5. _____ 

Now listen and repeat.

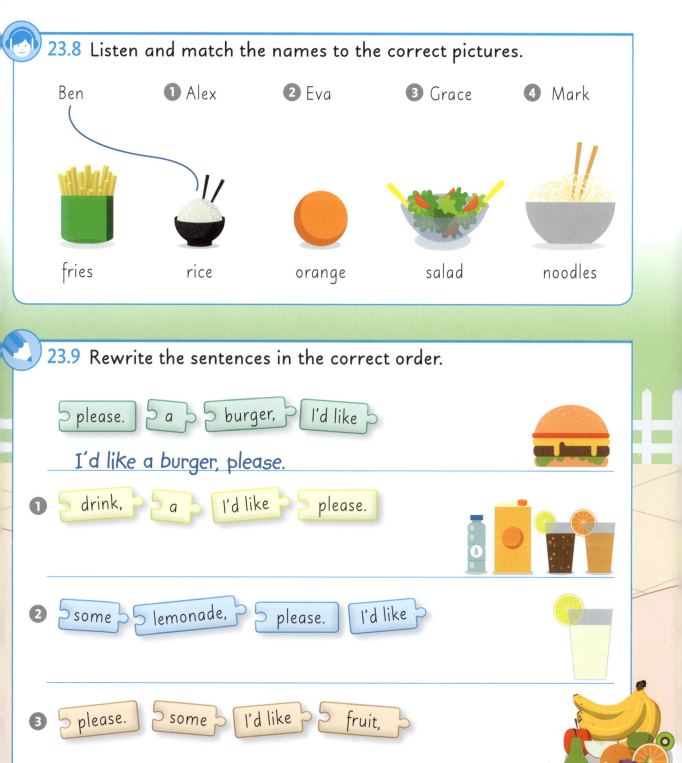

23.11 Listen and check off the correct answers.

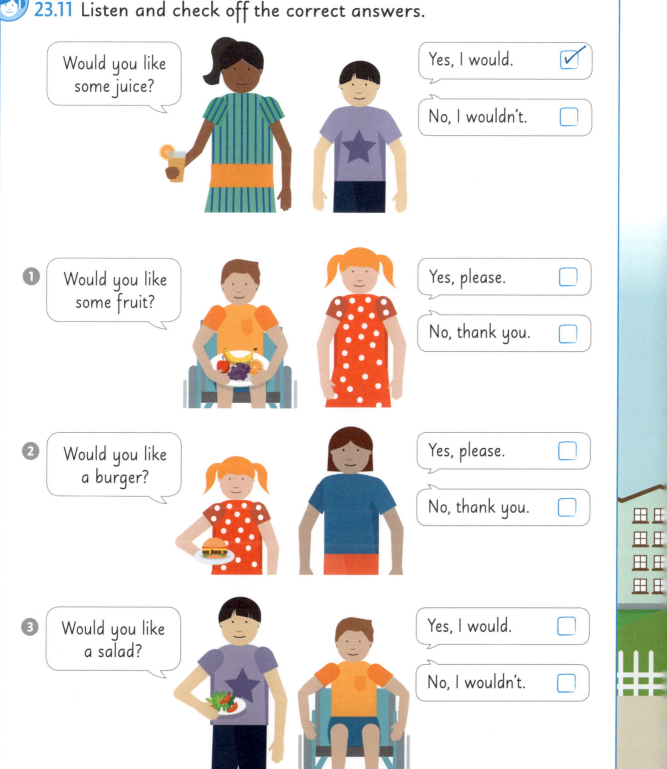

23.12 Listen, point, and repeat.

23.13 Listen and read.

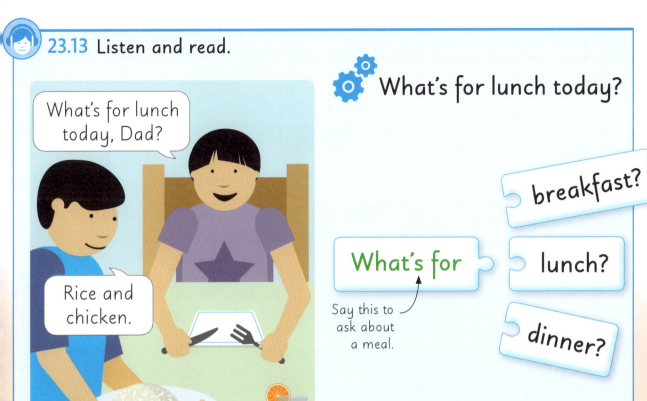

23.14 Listen and check off the correct pictures.

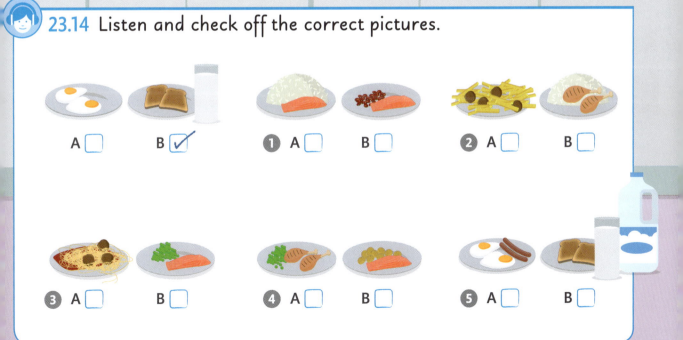

24 At the park

24.1 Listen, point, and repeat.
24.2 What are Sara and Max playing?

24.4 Look at the pictures and circle the correct words.

woman / (women)

① person / people

② boy / girl

③ child / children

④ man / men

⑤ woman / baby

Now listen and repeat.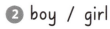

24.5 Find and circle the five words in the grid.

girl

~~child~~

people

kid

person

boy

p e r s o n
e c h i l d
o s i g e b
p b k i d o
l y r r d y
e o h l i h

202

24.6 Look at the pictures and write the letters in the correct order.

c d l i h

c h i l d

w n a o m

1 w _ _ _ _

m n e

2 m _ _

g r l i

3 g _ _ _

w n e m o

4 w _ _ _ _

k d s i

5 k _ _ _

Now listen and repeat.

24.9 Look at the pictures and write the correct words in the spaces.

woman's   ~~Sara's~~   boy's   Andy's   girl's   baby's

Sara's book is blue.

① The _____ ball is red.

② The _____ doll is pink.

③ The _____ dog is dirty.

④ _____ bike is yellow.

⑤ The _____ skirt is black.

Now listen and repeat.

24.10 Listen and read.

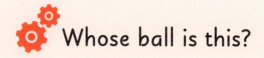

Whose ball is this?

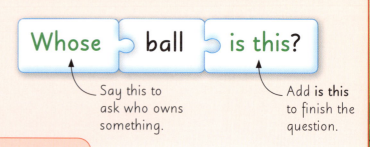

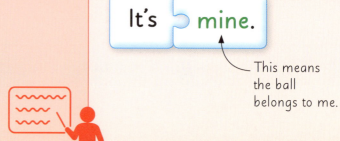

How it works
Whose is a question word used to ask who owns something.
Mine is an example of a possessive pronoun. These are used to say who owns something.

24.11 Listen and read.

24.12 Listen and write the correct answers in the spaces.

It's his.   ~~It's mine.~~   It's theirs.
It's ours.   It's hers.   It's yours.

Whose ball is this?

It's mine.

① Whose dog is this?

_____

② Whose bike is this?

_____

③ Whose boat is this?

_____

④ Whose lunch is this?

_____

⑤ Whose doll is this?

_____

207

25 My day

25.1 Listen, point, and repeat.
25.2 Who is Max calling?

25.3 Match the pictures to the correct sentences.

I study English.   I eat lunch.   I go home.

① I get up.

⑫ I go to sleep.

⑪ I eat dinner.

⑩ I go swimming.

⑨ I call my friend.

25.4 Listen and check off the correct pictures.

25.5 There are four sentences. Mark the beginning and end of each one and write them below.

I go home.

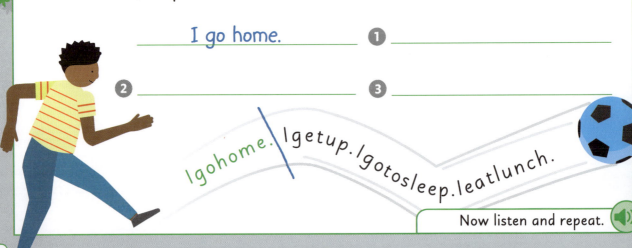

Now listen and repeat.

25.6 Look at the pictures and write the correct sentences in the spaces.

> I eat breakfast.   I eat lunch.   I study English.
> I brush my teeth.   I walk to school.   ~~I make my bed.~~

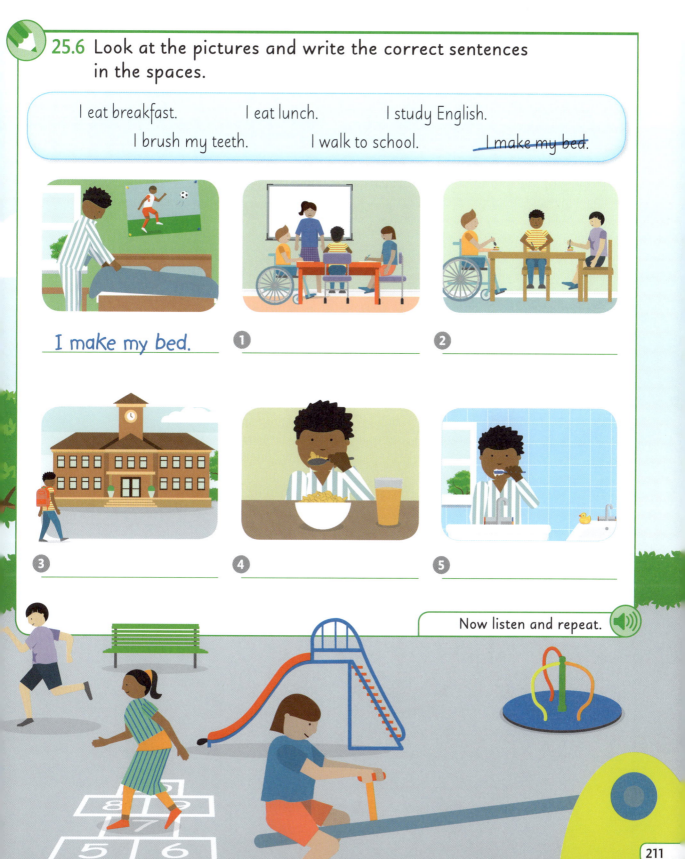

I make my bed.

① _____

② _____

③ _____

④ _____

⑤ _____

Now listen and repeat.

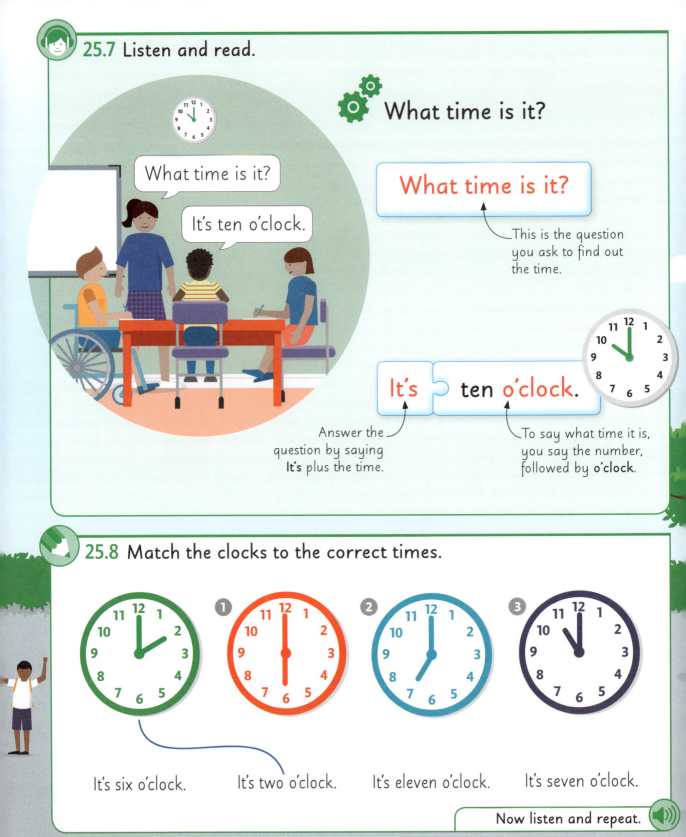

25.9 Listen, point, and repeat.

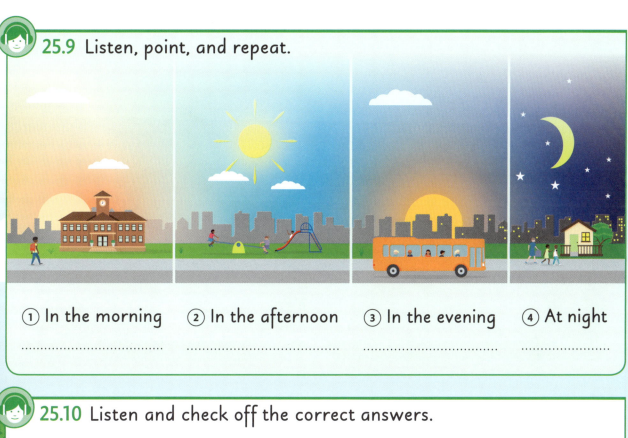

① In the morning   ② In the afternoon   ③ In the evening   ④ At night

25.10 Listen and check off the correct answers.

I go to school in the morning. ✓
I go to school at night. ☐

I study English at night. ☐
I study English in the afternoon. ☐

I call my friend in the evening. ☐
I call my friend in the afternoon. ☐

I go to sleep in the morning. ☐
I go to sleep at night. ☐

213

25.11 Listen and read.

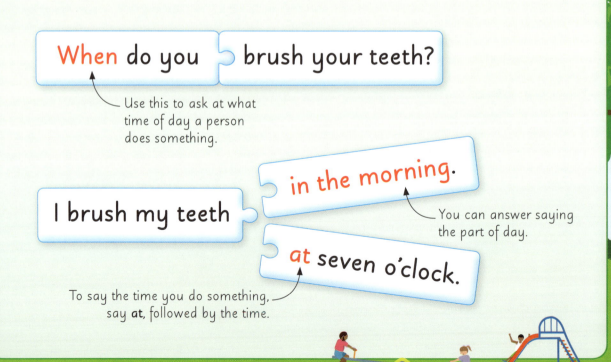

25.12 Read the sentences and write the correct words in the spaces.

> breakfast   go to sleep   six o'clock
> ~~morning~~   walk   we

In the __morning__, I wake up at seven o'clock.

1 I eat _____, and then I brush my teeth.

2 I _____ to school at eight o'clock.

3 In the afternoon, _____ study English.

4 I eat dinner at _____ with my family.

5 Then I _____ at seven o'clock.

Now listen and repeat.

25.14 Look at the pictures and circle the correct words.

Max **walk** / (**walks**) to school.

1 They **eat** / **eats** lunch.

2 We **go** / **goes** swimming.

3 She **study** / **studies** English.

4 She **get** / **gets** up.

5 Max **make** / **makes** his bed.

Now listen and repeat.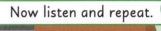

25.15 Listen, point, and repeat.

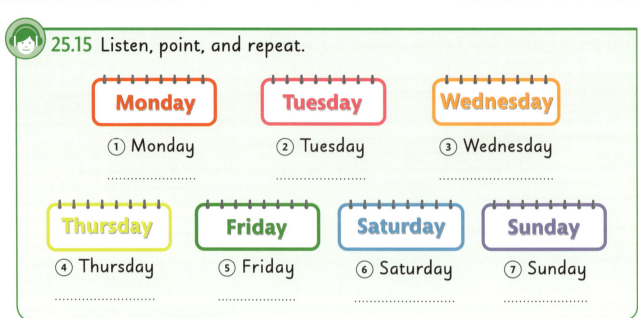

① Monday ② Tuesday ③ Wednesday
④ Thursday ⑤ Friday ⑥ Saturday ⑦ Sunday

25.16 Listen and read.

I go swimming on Fridays.

I go swimming | on Fridays.

Say **on**, followed by the day of the week with an **s** at its end.

So do I.

Say this if you also go swimming on Fridays.

I don't.

Say this if you don't go swimming on Fridays.

How it works

Use **at** when talking about what time you do something. Use **on** when talking about what days you do something.

25.17 Listen and check off the correct answers.

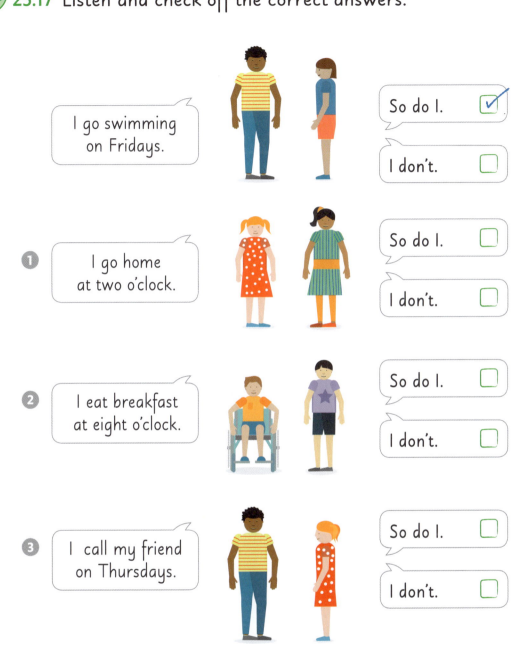

26 Review: Me and my day

 26.1 Listen and read.

I'm Andy. I have black hair and brown eyes. Today I'm wearing shorts and a T-shirt.

I like school. I go to school at 8 o'clock. In the morning, I study English. I eat rice and beans for lunch, and I drink juice. I go home at 3 o'clock. In the evening, I call my friends. I eat dinner at 6 o'clock, and I go to sleep at 7 o'clock.

26.2 Write about your day and draw what you're wearing.

I'm _____. I have _____ hair and _____ eyes. Today I'm wearing _____ and _____.

I _____ school. I go to school at _____. In the morning, I study _____. I eat _____ for lunch, and I drink _____. I go home at _____. In the evening, I _____. I eat dinner at _____, and I go to sleep at _____.

221

The alphabet

A1 The English alphabet has 26 letters. Listen to the audio and repeat each letter. Then listen to the song and sing.

Use a capital letter for the first letter of a sentence, people's names, and the days of the week.

Use lower-case letters the rest of the time.

Aa Bb Cc

Dd Ee Ff Gg Hh

Ii Jj Kk Ll Mm

Nn Oo Pp Qq Rr

Ss Tt Uu Vv Ww

Xx Yy Zz

Handwriting guide

A2 To practice writing English letters, start at the red dot and then follow the arrows.

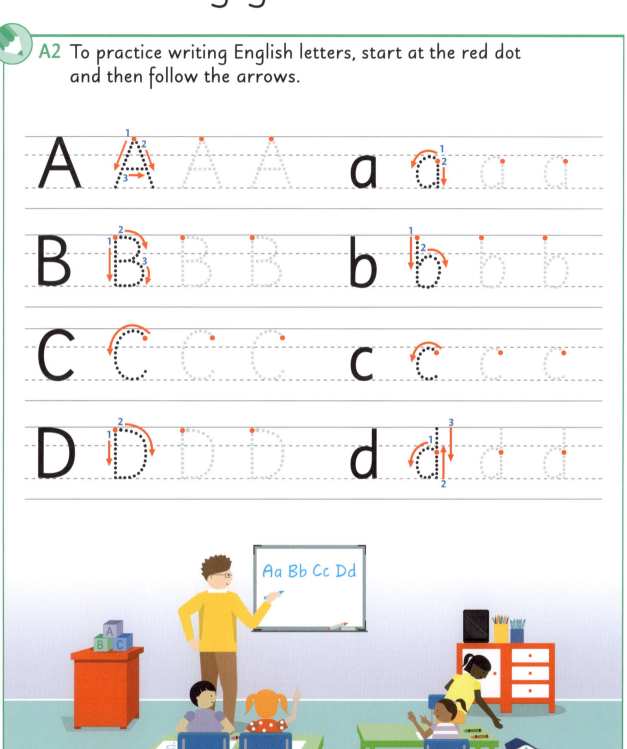

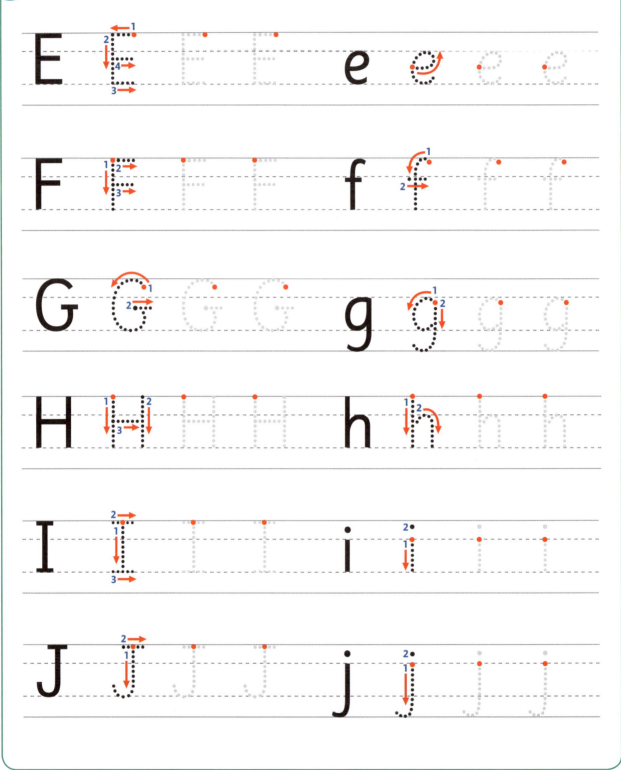

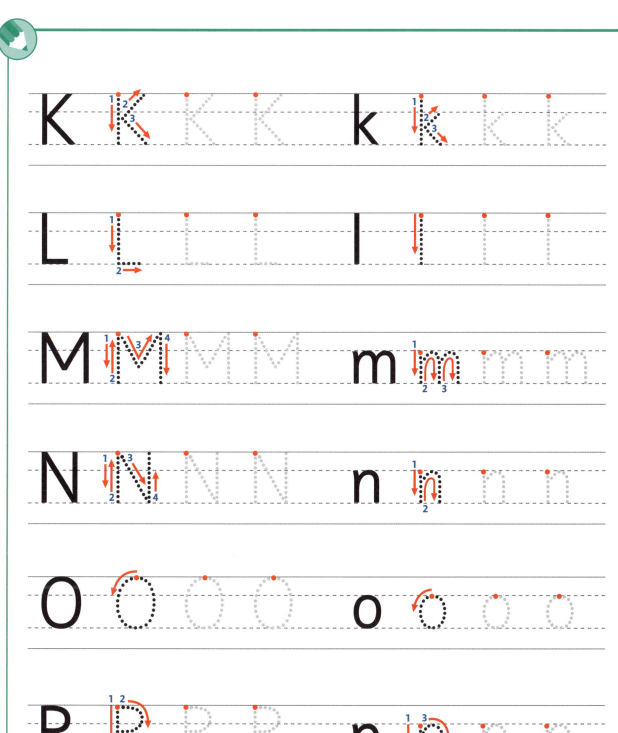

226

Grammar guide

G1 To be

Use **to be** to talk about yourself and describe people and things.

Positive	Negative
I am/I'm	I'm not
You are/You're	You aren't
He is/He's	He isn't
She is/She's	She isn't
It is/It's	It isn't
We are/We're	We aren't
You are/You're	You aren't
They are/They're	They aren't

G2 Have

Use **have** to talk about things you own.

Positive	Negative
I have	I don't have
You have	You don't have
He has	He doesn't have
She has	She doesn't have
It has	It doesn't have
We have	We don't have
You have	You don't have
They have	They don't have

G3 Can

Use **can** to talk about things you are able to do.

Positive	Negative
I can	I can't
You can	You can't
He can	He can't
She can	She can't
It can	It can't
We can	We can't
You can	You can't
They can	They can't

G4 The present simple

Use the present simple to talk about opinions or things people do every day.

Positive	Negative
I like	I don't like
You like	You don't like
He likes	He doesn't like
She likes	She doesn't like
It likes	It doesn't like
We like	We don't like
You like	You don't like
They like	They don't like

G5 The present continuous

Use the present continuous to talk about things people are doing now.

Positive	Negative
I am walking/I'm walking	I'm not walking
You are walking/You're walking	You aren't walking
He is walking/He's walking	He isn't walking
She is walking/She's walking	She isn't walking
It is walking/It's walking	It isn't walking
We are walking/We're walking	We aren't walking
You are walking/You're walking	You aren't walking
They are walking/They're walking	They aren't walking

G6 Question words

Use question words such as **what**, **who**, **where**, and **when** to ask questions that can't be answered with **yes** or **no**.

Question word	Example question	Example answer
What	What's that?	It's a crocodile.
Which	Which animal is big?	The dog is big.
Who	Who's that?	It's Ben.
Whose	Whose camera is this?	It's mine.
When	When do you go to school?	I go to school in the morning.
Where	Where's the cat?	It's under the table.
How	How old are you?	I'm nine years old.
How many	How many ducks are there?	There are five.
Why	Why do you like soccer?	It's fun!

G7 Irregular plurals

Most plurals are formed by adding an **s** or **es** to the end of a singular noun. However, some plurals are irregular and are spelled differently or don't change at all.

Singular	Plural
mouse	mice
tooth	teeth
foot	feet
child	children
woman	women
man	men
person	people
sheep	sheep
fish	fish

G8 Prepositions of place

Use prepositions of place to say where things are.

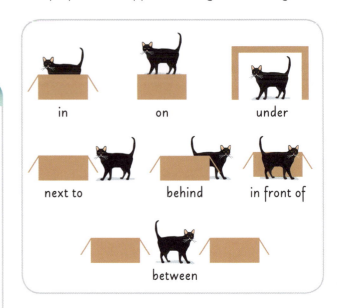

in   on   under
next to   behind   in front of
between

G9 This, that, these, those

Use **this**, **that**, **these**, and **those** to point things out.

	Singular	Plural
Near to you	This dog	These dogs
Far from you	That dog	Those dogs

G10 Pronouns, possessive adjectives, and possessive pronouns

Pronouns can replace nouns (names of people, places, and things) in a sentence.

Subject pronoun	Object pronoun	Possessive adjective	Possessive pronoun
Subject pronouns replace the person or thing that is doing an action. Example: Is **she** happy?	Object pronouns replace the person or thing that is having an action done to it. Example: I like **him**.	Possessive adjectives are used before a noun to say who something belongs to. Example: It's **my** book.	When you use a possessive pronoun, you don't need to use the noun. Example: It's **theirs**.
I	me	my	mine
you	you	your	yours
he	him	his	his
she	her	her	hers
it	it	its	its
we	us	our	ours
you	you	your	yours
they	them	their	theirs

G11 Conjunctions

Conjunctions, such as **and**, **but**, and **or**, are words that join two statements together.

Use **and** to join words in a positive statement.

I like oranges **and** bananas.

Use **but** to join a positive statement and a negative statement together.

I like oranges **but** I don't like bananas.

Use **or** to join words in a negative statement.

I don't like oranges **or** bananas.

G12 Common verbs

A verb is a word that describes an action.
This table shows some common English verbs.

Verb	Example sentence
give	Please **give** me that book.
hold	My baby brother can't **hold** a pen.
put	I **put** my toys in my toy box.
see	I can **see** an airplane in the sky!
stop	Where does this train **stop**?
talk	I **talk** to my friends at school.
tell	Can you **tell** me where the park is?
try	I **try** to speak English every day.

231

G13 Instructions

When you learn English or take a test, you might see these words in instructions.

Verbs

Nouns

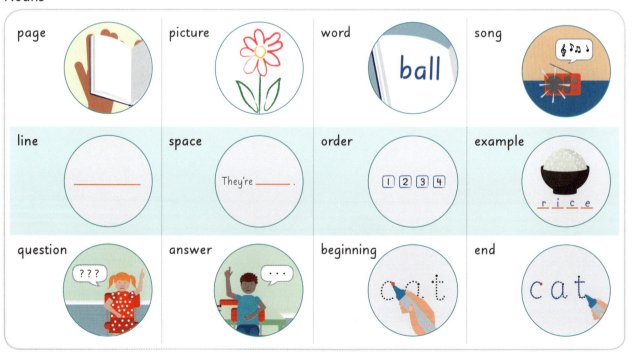

G14 Useful expressions

These expressions are useful for greeting people, saying goodbye, being polite, asking for information, or showing that you're happy.

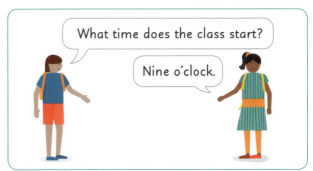

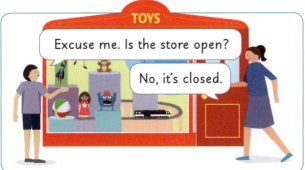

Answers

1

1.3
1. Sofia
2. Max
3. Ben
4. Maria
5. Sara

1.6
1. eight
2. six
3. ten
4. nine
5. five

1.8
1. I'm **seven** years old.
2. I'm **six** years old.
3. I'm **10** years old.

2

2.2
1. classmate
2. book
3. teacher
4. board

2.4
1. listen
2. answer
3. sit down
4. add
5. pick up

2.5
1. B
2. B
3. B
4. B
5. B

2.7
1. What's **his** name?
2. **His** name's Hugo.
3. What's **her** name?

3

3.2
1. draw
2. read
3. count
4. spell

3.5
1. Let's count!
2. Let's write!
3. Let's read!
4. Let's draw!
5. Let's play!

3.6
1. Let's **count**!
2. Let's **write**!
3. Let's **read**!

3.8
1. fifteen
2. twenty
3. eighteen
4. thirteen

3.10

1 pens   2 teacher   3 chairs

4

4.2

six pencils

4.3

1 crayon   2 eraser   3 pencil
4 watch   5 pen

4.4

1 blue   2 brown   3 red
4 gray   5 purple

4.5

1 A   2 B   3 A   4 B

4.6

1 crayon   2 white   3 black
4 green   5 apple

4.8

1 It's an eraser.
2 It's an apple.
3 It's a watch.

4.10

1 They're **notepads**.
2 They're **rulers**.
3 They're **crayons**.
4 They're **erasers**.

4.13

1 purple   2 pink   3 orange
4 blue   5 green

4.14

1 It's yellow.
2 It's black.
3 It's purple.
4 It's red.

5

5.2

blue

5.3

1 monkey   2 tiger   3 hippo
4 whale   5 parrot

5.4

1 crocodile
2 bear
3 frog

235

5.5
① lion ② snake ③ lizard
④ penguin

5.6
① B ② A ③ A

5.9
① It's a **giraffe**.
② It's a **bear**.
③ It's a **crocodile**.

5.11
① A ② B ③ B
④ B ⑤ A

5.13
① penguin ② parrot ③ lizard
④ zebra ⑤ snake

6

6.2

6.3
① my brother ② my aunt
③ my sister ④ my cousin

6.4
① my dad ② my mom
③ my sister ④ my brother

6.5
① uncle ② grandma
③ brother ④ mom ⑤ father

6.6
① cousin ② mother ③ sister
④ grandpa ⑤ aunt ⑥ dad

6.8
① Who's this? ② Who's this?
③ Who's that?

6.10
① No, he isn't. ② No, she isn't.
③ Yes, she is.

6.13
① He's a vet.
② She's a firefighter.
③ He's a farmer.
④ She's a doctor.
⑤ She's a police officer.

7

7.2

7.3
1. ball 2. desk 3. doll
4. car 5. lamp

7.4
1. teddy bear
2. camera
3. baseball bat
4. tennis racket

7.5
1. They're chairs.
2. They're dolls.
3. It's a skateboard.
4. It's a toy box.
5. It's a rug.

7.6
1. camera
2. poster
3. chair
4. car
5. lamp

7.8
1. These are my dolls.
2. These are my lamps.
3. This is my rug.

7.9
1. **That's** my poster.
2. **That's** my skateboard.
3. **Those are** my cars.

7.11
1. Max 2. Max 3. Sofia
4. Max 5. Sofia

7.13
1. Yes, I do.
2. Yes, I do.
3. No, I don't.

9

9.2

9.3
① cold　② sad
③ tired　④ happy

9.4
① excited　② hot　③ scared

9.5
① sad　② happy
③ cold　④ tired

9.6
① hungry　② happy　③ scared
④ sad　⑤ thirsty

9.9
① B　② A　③ A

9.10
① They're happy.
② We're hungry.
③ They're excited.

9.12
① No, we aren't.
② No, they aren't.
③ Yes, they are.

10

10.2
six fish

10.3
① cat　② tortoise
③ rabbit　④ dog

10.5
① cat　② mouse　③ dog

10.6
① nice
② young
③ big
④ beautiful
⑤ scary

10.7

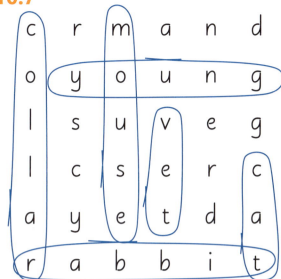

10.10
① tortoise ② cat
③ dog ④ rabbit

10.11
① Ben has a **mouse**.
② She has a **dog**.
③ Sara has a **fish**.

10.13
① No, she doesn't.
② No, he doesn't.
③ Yes, he does.

10.14
① A ② B ③ B

10.16
① Bonzo ② Lee ③ Ted
④ Rex ⑤ Meg

11

11.2
Sara

11.3
① head ② mouth
③ hand ④ long hair

11.4
① arm ② toes ③ eye

11.5
① fingers ② hair ③ teeth
④ toes ⑤ mouth ⑥ ear

11.6
① hair ② nose ③ face
④ teeth ⑤ body

11.8
① B ② B ③ B
④ A ⑤ A

239

11.10
1. No, it doesn't.
2. Yes, it does.
3. Yes, it does.
4. No, it doesn't.

11.12
1. **Wave** your arms!
2. **Point** one finger!
3. **Move** your feet!

12

12.2
five cars

12.3
1. bus
2. truck
3. bike

12.4
1. school
2. hospital
3. park
4. helicopter
5. bike
6. train

12.5
1. bus
2. motorcycle
3. airplane
4. hospital

12.6
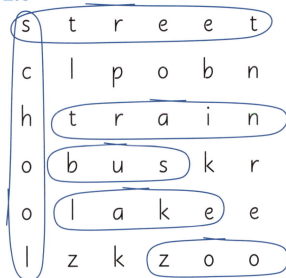

12.9
1. **There are** two trucks.
2. **There's** a school.
3. **There's** a zoo.
4. **There are** four cars.
5. **There are** three boats.

12.12
1. It's **next to** the store.
2. It's **in front of** the hospital.
3. It's **behind** the school.
4. It's **between** the park and the store.

12.14
1. A
2. B
3. A

13

13.2
the kitchen

13.3
1 kitchen 2 bathroom 3 bedroom

13.4
1 It's a bookcase. 2 It's a door.
3 It's a couch. 4 It's a television.
5 It's a refrigerator.

13.5
1 bookcase 2 table 3 flowers
4 clock 5 armchair 6 mat

13.6
1 hall 2 plants 3 window
4 lights 5 wall

13.9
1 B 2 A 3 B

13.12
1 No, there isn't. 2 Yes, there is.
3 Yes, there is. 4 No, there isn't.
5 No, there isn't.

13.14
1 No, there aren't. 2 Yes, there are.
3 Yes, there are. 4 No, there aren't.
5 Yes, there are.

15

15.2
11 sheep

15.3
1 bee 2 horse 3 barn
4 cow 5 goat

15.4
1 tail 2 tractor 3 barn
4 the sun 5 donkey

15.5
1 goat 2 horse
3 duck 4 tree

15.6
1 chicken 2 field 3 bee
4 pond 5 goat 6 tree

15.8
1 There are three. 2 There are four.
3 There's one.

15.10
1. They're in front of the barn.
2. They're under the tree.
3. They're in the field.
4. They're in the barn.
5. They're next to the pond.

15.13
This is my farm. My cow **is** under the tree. There ① **are** four ducks ② **in** the pond. The three chickens ③ **are** next to the horse. The donkey ④ **is** in the field, and five sheep ⑤ **are** in front of the barn.

16

16.2

16.3
1. ice hockey
2. tennis
3. basketball
4. badminton

16.4
1. table tennis
2. basketball
3. baseball

16.5
1. ice hockey
2. badminton
3. swimming
4. soccer

16.7
1. B
2. A
3. A
4. B
5. B

16.8
1. catch
2. swim
3. throw
4. kick
5. bounce

16.10
1. I **can** catch a ball.
2. I **can't** play ice hockey.
3. I **can** hit a ball.
4. I **can** swim.
5. I **can't** play table tennis.

16.12
1. Yes, **I can**.
2. **Can you** play baseball?
3. No, **I can't**.

16.14
1. Yes, she can.
2. No, she can't.
3. Yes, he can.

17

17.2

17.3
① meat ② onions ③ kiwis ④ lemons ⑤ pears

17.4
① B ② A ③ A ④ B

17.5
① lime ② orange ③ carrot ④ fish ⑤ coconut

17.6
① yellow ② brown ③ red ④ green ⑤ purple

17.9
① I **don't like** watermelons.
② I **like** apples.
③ I **like** lemons and limes.
④ I **don't like** carrots or onions.
⑤ I **don't like** tomatoes.

17.11
① No, **I don't**.
② Yes, **I do**.
③ Do you **like** mangoes?

17.13
① May I have **a** banana, please?
② May I have **an** orange, please?
③ May I have **some** vegetables, please?

18

18.2
8 stars

18.3
① puppet ② the moon ③ robot

18.4
① board game ② car ③ ball

18.5
① robot
② rocket
③ alien

243

18.6
① It's a **monster**.
② They're **stars**.
③ It's an **action figure**.

18.8
Sofia likes **cars**. Her cousin Eva doesn't like ① **video games**. Ben likes ② **rockets**, but his friend Sam doesn't like ③ **trains**.

18.9
① Hugo **doesn't like** puppets.
② Lucy **doesn't like** dolls.
③ Emma **likes** monsters.

18.11
① No, she doesn't.   ② No, he doesn't.
③ Yes, she does.   ④ Yes, he does.
⑤ No, she doesn't.

18.12
① No, he doesn't.
② Does she like dolls?
③ Yes, she does.

18.15
① I don't.
② Me too!
③ I don't.

19

19.2

19.3
① dance   ② sing
③ draw pictures ④ take photos

19.4
① B   ② A   ③ A
④ B   ⑤ A

19.5
① sing   ② take photos
③ ride a bike   ④ play the piano
⑤ paint

19.7
① singing   ② drawing
③ reading   ④ watching soccer

244

19.8
1 I enjoy taking photos.
2 I don't like riding a bike.
3 I like watching soccer.

19.10
1 Yes, I do. 2 No, I don't.
3 No, I don't. 4 Yes, I do.

21

21.2
blue

21.3
1 bag 2 jacket 3 hat

21.4
1 watch 2 dress 3 glasses
4 boot 5 baseball cap

21.5
1 B 2 A 3 A 4 B

21.6
1 It's a watch.
2 It's a jacket.
3 It's a sock.

4 It's a T-shirt.
5 It's a shoe.

21.9
1 B 2 A 3 A 4 B 5 B

21.11
1 No, I'm not. 2 Yes, I am.
3 Yes, I am.

21.13
1 **What** beautiful boots!
2 **What a** dirty sock!
3 **What** nice glasses!
4 **What a** nice shirt!
5 **What a** big purse!

22

22.2
three balls

22.3
1 drink juice
2 play soccer
3 throw a ball
4 listen to music
5 read a book

245

22.4

1. It's a shovel.
2. It's a shell.
3. It's a seagull.
4. It's a ship.
5. It's a bucket.

22.5

1. A
2. A
3. A
4. B
5. B

22.6

1. bucket
2. sand
3. run
4. shell
5. swim

22.8

1. She isn't swimming.
2. He isn't flying a kite.
3. She's drinking juice.

22.9

1. swimming
2. playing soccer
3. flying a kite
4. fishing

22.11

1. No, she isn't.
2. Yes, she is.
3. Yes, he is.

23

23.2

a burger

23.3

1. pie
2. salad
3. cake

23.4

1. orange
2. chocolate
3. juice
4. rice
5. salad

23.5

1. B
2. B
3. A

23.6

1. fries
2. fruit
3. sausages
4. burger
5. lemonade

23.8

1. fries
2. salad
3. noodles
4. orange

23.9

1. I'd like a drink, please.
2. I'd like some lemonade, please.
3. I'd like some fruit, please.

23.11
1. No, thank you.
2. Yes, please.
3. Yes, I would.

23.14
1. B 2. B 3. A 4. B 5. A

24

24.2
tennis

24.3
1. man
2. boy
3. men

24.4
1. people
2. boy
3. children
4. man
5. baby

24.5
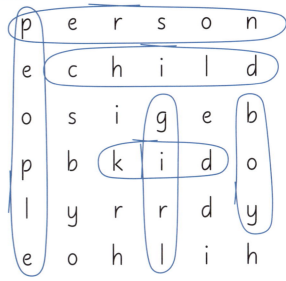

24.6
1. woman 2. men 3. girl
4. women 5. kids

24.8
1. red bike
2. yellow bag
3. orange bike
4. green bike

24.9
1. The **girl's** ball is red.
2. The **baby's** doll is pink.
3. The **boy's** dog is dirty.
4. **Andy's** bike is yellow.
5. The **woman's** skirt is black.

24.12
1 It's theirs. 2 It's his.
3 It's hers. 4 It's ours.
5 It's yours.

25

25.2
Ben

25.3
1 I study English.
2 I eat lunch.
3 I get up.
4 I go to sleep.
5 I make my bed.

25.4
1 A 2 B 3 A 4 A 5 B

25.5
1 I get up.
2 I go to sleep.
3 I eat lunch.

25.6
1 I study English.
2 I eat lunch.
3 I walk to school.

4 I eat breakfast.
5 I brush my teeth.

25.8
1 It's six o'clock.
2 It's seven o'clock.
3 It's eleven o'clock.

25.10
1 I study English in the afternoon.
2 I call my friend in the evening.
3 I go to sleep at night.

25.12
1 I eat **breakfast**, and then I brush my teeth.
2 I **walk** to school at eight o'clock.
3 In the afternoon, **we** study English.
4 I eat dinner at **6 o'clock** with my family.
5 Then I **go to sleep** at seven o'clock.

25.14
1 eat 2 go 3 studies
4 gets 5 makes

25.17
1 I don't.
2 So do I.
3 I don't.

Grammar index

Each entry is followed by the number of the unit it appears in. Entries that appear in the **Grammar guide** have a **G** before them (for example, **G3**).

A

adjectives **2, 6, 9, 21, G10**
and **17, G11**
apostrophes **24**
articles **4, 5, 6, 17**

B

be (is/are) **1, 4, 5, 6, 9, 15, 21, 21, 22, 25, G1**
but **G11**

C

can **16, G3**
common verbs **G12**
conjunctions **17, G11**
countable nouns **23**

D

do **17, 18**

G

greetings **1**

H

have **7, 10, 11, G2**
how? **1, G6**
how are you? **1**
how many? **15, G6**
how old are you? **1**

I

indefinite article **17**
instructions **G13**
irregular plurals **10, 11, 17, G7**

L

let's **3**
like+noun **17, 18**
like+verb+ing **19**

M, O

may **17**
me too **18**
mine **24**
one **10**
or **17, G11**

P

plurals **3, 10, 11, 17, G7**
possessive adjectives **1, 2, 6, G10**
possessive pronouns **24, G10**
prepositions **12, 13, 15, G8**
present continuous **21, 22, G5**
present simple **9, 17, 18, 25, G4**
pronouns **24, G10**

Q

question words **4, 5, 6, 10, 12, 15, 24, G6**

S

short forms **1**
singular and plural **3**
so do I **25**
some **17, 23**

T

telling the time **25**
that **5, 6, 7, 18, G9**
there is/there are **12, 13, 15**
these **4, 7, 25, G9**
this **4, 6, 7, 24, 25, G9**
those **5, 7, 18, G9**
to be *see be*
to have *see have*
to like *see like*

U

uncountable nouns **23**
useful expressions **G14**

W

what? **1, 2, 4, 5, G6**
what (a/an) **21**
when? **25, G6**
where? **12, G6**
which? **10, G6**
who? **6, G6**
whose? **24, G6**
why? **G6**
would like **23**

Word list

Each word is followed by the number of the unit it is taught in. Words that appear in the **Grammar guide** have a **G** before them (for example, **G3**).

KEY

adj	adjective
exp	expression
int	question word
n	noun
num	number
pl	plural
prep	preposition
pron	pronoun
v	verb

A

action figure *n* **18**
add *v* **2**
afternoon *n* **25**
airplane *n* **12**
airport *n* **12**
alien *n* **18**
alphabet *n* **2**
and *conj* **17, G11**
animal *n* **5**
answer *n* **G13**
answer *v* **2**
apartment block *n* **12**
apple *n* **4, 17**
arm *n* **11**

armchair *n* **13**
ask *v* **2**
at night *exp* **25**
aunt *n* **6**

B

baby (pl babies) *n* **24**
badminton *n* **16**
bag *n* **21, 24**
ball *n* **4, 7, 18, 22**
balloon *n* **18**
banana *n* **17**
barn *n* **15**
baseball *n* **16**
baseball bat *n* **7**
baseball cap *n* **21**
basketball *n* **16**
bathroom *n* **13**
bathtub *n* **13**
be (is/are) *v* **1, 4, 5, 6, 9, 15, 21, 22, 25, G1**
beach (pl beaches) *n* **22**
bean *n* **23**
bear *n* **5**
beautiful *adj* **10, 21**
bed *n* **7, 25**
bedroom *n* **13**
bee *n* **15**
beginning *n* **G13**
behind *prep* **12, G8**
between *prep* **12, G8**
big *adj* **10, 21**
bike *n* **12, 19**
bird *n* **5**
black *adj* **4**

blue *adj* **4**
board *n* **2**
board game *n* **18**
boat *n* **12**
body (pl bodies) *n* **11**
book *n* **2, 4, 22**
bookcase *n* **13**
bookstore *n* **12**
book pack *n* **4**
boot *n* **21**
bounce *v* **16**
boy *n* **24**
bread *n* **23**
breakfast *n* **23, 25**
brother *n* **6**
brown *adj* **4**
brush your teeth *v* **25**
bucket *n* **22**
burger *n* **23**
bus (pl buses) *n* **12**
but *conj* **G11**
bye *exp* **G14**

C

cake *n* **23**
call *v* **25**
camera *n* **7**
can *v* **16, G3**
car *n* **7, 12, 18**
carrot *n* **17**
cat *n* **10**
catch *v* **16**
chair *n* **2, 7, 13**
check off *v* **G13**
chef *n* **6**

chicken *n* **15, 23**
child (pl children) *n* **24**
children *n* **24**
chocolate *n* **23**
circle *v* **G13**
clap *v* **11**
classmate *n* **2**
classroom *n* **3**
clean *adj* **10, 21**
clock *n* **13, 25**
close *v* **2**
clothes *n* **21**
coconut *n* **17**
cold *adj* **9**
collar *n* **10**
color *n* **4**
color in *v* **G13**
computer *n* **7**
cool! *exp* **G14**
couch *n* **13**
count *v* **3, G13**
cousin *n* **6**
cow *n* **15**
crayon *n* **4**
crocodile *n* **5**
cross out *v* **G13**
cupboard *n* **2**

D

dad *n* **6**
dance *v* **19**
day *n* **25**
desk *n* **7**
dining room *n* **13**
dinner *n* **23, 25**

dirty *adj* **10, 21**
do you know? *exp* **G14**
do you want? *exp* **G14**
doctor *n* **6**
dog *n* **10**
doll *n* **7, 18**
donkey *n* **15**
don't worry *exp* **G14**
door *n* **13**
draw *v* **3**
dress (pl dresses) *n* **21**
drink *n* **23**
duck *n* **15**

E

ear *n* **11**
eat *v* **22, 23, 25**
egg *n* **23**
eight *num* **1**
eighteen *num* **3**
elephant *n* **5**
eleven *num* **3**
end *n* **G13**
enjoy *v* **19**
eraser *n* **4**
evening *n* **25**
example *n* **G13**
excited *adj* **9**
excuse me *exp* **G14**
eye *n* **11**

F

face *n* **11**
fair *n* **9**

family (pl families) *n* **6**
fantastic! *exp* **G14**
farm *n* **15**
farmer *n* **6**
father *n* **6**
favorite *adj* **5**
feet *n* **11**
field *n* **15**
fifteen *num* **3**
find *v* **2**
fine *adj* **1**
finger *n* **11**
fire station *n* **12**
firefighter *n* **6**
fish (pl fish) *n* **10, 17, 23**
fish *v* **22**
five *num* **1**
floor *n* **13**
flower *n* **13**
fly a kite *v* **22**
food market *n* **17**
foot (pl feet) *n* **11**
four *num* **1**
fourteen *num* **3**
Friday *n* **25**
friend *n* **1, 25**
fries *n* **23**
frog *n* **5**
fruit *n* **17, 23**

G

game *n* **18**
garden *n* **13**
get up *v* **25**
giraffe *n* **5**

251

girl *n* **24**
give *v* **G12**
glasses *n* **21**
go home *v* **25**
go swimming *v* **25**
go to sleep *v* **25**
goat *n* **15**
good morning *exp* **G14**
goodbye *exp* **G14**
grandfather/grandpa *n* **6**
grandmother/grandma *n* **6**
grape *n* **17**
green *adj* **4**
gray *adj* **4**
guitar *n* **19**

H
hair *n* **11**
hall *n* **13**
hand *n* **11**
happy *adj* **9**
hat *n* **21**
have *v* **7, 10, 11, 17, G2**
he *pron* **6**
head *n* **11**
helicopter *n* **12**
hello *exp* **1, G14**
her *adj* **2, G10**
hers *pron* **24**
hi *exp* **1**
hippo *n* **5**
his *adj* **2, G10**
his *pron* **24**
hit *v* **16**
hobby (pl hobbies) *n* **19**

hold *v* **G12**
home *n* **13, 25**
hooray! *exp* **G14**
horse *n* **15**
hospital *n* **12**
hot *adj* **9**
house *n* **12**
how? *int* **1, G6**
how many? *int* **15, G6**
hungry *adj* **9**

I, J, K
ice cream *n* **22**
ice hockey *n* **16**
I'm sorry *exp* **G14**
in *prep* **13, 15, G8**
in front of *prep* **12, G8**
in the afternoon *exp* **25**
in the evening *exp* **25**
in the morning *exp* **25**
jacket *n* **21**
jeans *n* **21**
jellyfish (pl jellyfish) *n* **22**
juice *n* **22, 23**
jump *v* **16**
keyboard *n* **7**
kick *v* **16**
kid *n* **24**
kitchen *n* **13**
kite *n* **22**
kiwi *n* **17**

L
lake *n* **12**
lamp *n* **7**
leg *n* **11**
lemon *n* **17**
lemonade *n* **23**
letter *n* **2**
light *n* **13**
like *v* **17, 18, 19, 23**
lime *n* **17**
line *n* **G13**
lion *n* **5**
listen *v* **2, G13**
listen to music *v* **22**
live *v* **12**
living room *n* **13**
lizard *n* **5**
long *adj* **11**
look (at) *v* **2, G13**
love *v* **18, G14**
lunch *n* **23, 25**
lunchtime *n* **23**

M
make my bed *v* **25**
man (pl men) *n* **24**
mango (pl mangoes) *n* **17**
mat *n* **13**
match *v* **G13**
may *v* **17**
me *pron* **6**
meat *n* **17**
meatball *n* **23**
men *n* **24**
milk *n* **23**

252

mine *pron* 24
mirror *n* 13
mom *n* 6
Monday *n* 25
monkey *n* 5
monster *n* 18
moon, the *n* 18
morning *n* 25
mother *n* 6
motorcycle *n* 12
mouse (pl mice) *n* 7, 10
mouth *n* 11
move *v* 11
music *n* 22
my *adj* 1, 4, 5, 6, 7, 11, 13, 21, 25, G10

N
name *n* 1, 2
next to *prep* 12, G8
nice *adj* 10, 21
night *n* 25
nine *num* 1
nineteen *num* 3
no, thank you *exp* 23
noodles *n* 23
nose *n* 11
notepad *n* 4
number *n* 2

O
o'clock *adv* 25, G14
ocean *n* 22
oh dear *exp* G14

old *adj* 10
on *prep* 13, G8
one *num* 1
one *pron* 10
onion *n* 17
open *v* 2
or *conj* 17, G11
orange *adj* 4
orange *n* 17, 23
order *n* G13
our *adj* G10
ours *pron* 24

P
page *n* G13
paint *v* 3, 19
pants *n* 21
paper *n* 4
pardon? *int* G14
park *n* 12, 24
parrot *n* 5
party (pl parties) *n* 21
pasta *n* 23
pea *n* 23
pear *n* 17
pen *n* 2, 4
pencil *n* 2, 4
penguin *n* 5
people *n* 24
person (pl people) *n* 24
pet *n* 10
photo *n* 19
piano *n* 19
pick up *v* 2
picture *n* 19, G13

pie *n* 23
pig *n* 15
pineapple *n* 17
pink *adj* 4
plant *n* 13
play *v* 3, 16
play a musical instrument *v* 19
play a sport *v* 16
playground *n* 2
please *adv* 17, 23, G14
point *v* 11, G13
polar bear *n* 5
police officer *n* 6
pond *n* 15
poster *n* 7
potato (pl potatoes) *n* 17, 23
puppet *n* 18
purple *adj* 4
purse *n* 21
put *v* G12

Q
question *n* G13

R
rabbit *n* 10
read *v* 3, 19, G13
really *adv* 9
red *adj* 4
refrigerator *n* 13
repeat *v* G13
rice *n* 23
ride a bike *v* 19

253

robot *n* **11, 18**
rocket *n* **18**
room *n* **7, 13**
rug *n* **7**
ruler *n* **4**
run *v* **16, 22**

S

sad *adj* **9**
salad *n* **23**
sand *n* **22**
Saturday *n* **25**
sausage *n* **23**
scared *adj* **9**
scary *adj* **10**
school *n* **2, 12, 25**
seagull *n* **22**
see *v* **G12**
see you! *exp* **G14**
seven *num* **1**
seventeen *num* **3**
she *pron* **6**
sheep (pl sheep) *n* **15**
shell *n* **22**
ship *n* **22**
shirt *n* **21**
shoe *n* **21**
short hair *n* **11**
shorts *n* **21**
shovel *n* **22**
show *v* **2**
sing *v* **19**
sister *n* **6**
sit down *v* **2**
six *num* **1**

sixteen *num* **3**
skateboard *n* **7**
skateboard *v* **19**
skirt *n* **21**
sleep, go to *v* **25**
small *adj* **10**
snake *n* **5**
soccer *n* **16, 19, 22**
sock *n* **21**
song *n* **G13**
sorry, I'm *exp* **G14**
space *n* **G13**
spell *v* **3**
spider *n* **10**
sport *n* **16**
stand up *v* **2**
star *n* **18**
stop *v* **G12**
street *n* **12**
store *n* **12**
study *v* **25**
study English *v* **25**
sun, the *n* **15**
Sunday *n* **25**
surf *v* **22**
swim *v* **16, 22**
swimming *n* **16**

T

table *n* **13**
table tennis *n* **16**
tablet *n* **2**
tail *n* **15**
take photos *v* **19**
talk *v* **G12**

teacher *n* **2, 6**
teddy bear *n* **7, 18**
teeth *n* **11, 25**
television/TV *n* **13**
tell *v* **G12**
ten *num* **1**
tennis *n* **16**
tennis racket *n* **7**
thank you/thanks *exp* **1, 23**
that *pron* **5, 6, 7, 18, G9**
their *adj* **G10**
the moon *n* **18**
the sun *n* **15**
theirs *pron* **23**
these *pron* **4, 7, 25, G9**
thing *n* **4**
thirsty *adj* **9**
thirteen *num* **3**
this *pron* **4, 6, 7, G9**
those *pron* **5, 7, G9**
three *num* **1**
throw *v* **16, 22**
Thursday *n* **25**
tiger *n* **5**
time *n* **25**
tired *adj* **9**
toe *n* **11**
tomato (pl tomatoes) *n* **17**
tooth (pl teeth) *n* **11**
tortoise *n* **10**
touch *v* **11**
town *n* **12**
toy *n* **7**
toy box (pl toy boxes) *n* **7**
toy store *n* **18**
tractor *n* **15**

train *n* **12, 18**
tree *n* **15**
truck *n* **12**
try *v* **G12**
T-shirt *n* **21**
Tuesday *n* **25**
TV *n* **13**
twelve *num* **3**
twenty *num* **3**
two *num* **1**

U

uncle *n* **6**
under *prep* **13, 15, G8**

V

vegetable *n* **17**
very *adv* **9**
vet *n* **6, 10**
video game *n* **18**

W

wake up *v* **25**
walk *v* **25**
walk to school *v* **25**
wall *n* **13**
want *v* **G14**
watch (pl watches) *n* **4, 21**
watch soccer *v* **19**
water *n* **23**
watermelon *n* **17**
wave *v* **11**
wear *v* **21**
Wednesday *n* **25**
whale *n* **5**
what? *int* **1, 2, 4, 5, G6**
what time? *int* **25, G14**
when? *int* **25, G6**
where? *int* **12, G6**
which? *int* **10, G6**
white *adj* **4**
who? *int* **6, G6**
whose? *int* **24, G6**
why? *int* **G6**

window *n* **13**
woman (pl women) *n* **24**
women *n* **24**
word *n* **G13**
worry, don't *exp* **G14**
would *v* **23**
write *v* **3, G13**

Y

year *n* **1**
yellow *adj* **4**
yes, please *exp* **23, G14**
young *adj* **10**
your *adj* **5, 6, G10**
yours *pron* **24**

Z

zebra *n* **5**
zoo *n* **12**

Acknowledgments

The publisher would like to thank:

Rishi Bryan and Soma B. Chowdhury for editorial assistance; Renata Latipova, Gus Scott, Francis Wong, and Steve Woosnam-Savage for design and illustration assistance; Sourabh Challariya, Chhaya Sajwan, and Arunesh Talapatra for design assistance; Kayla Dugger, Lori Hand, and Steph Noviss for proofreading; Tim Woolf for songwriting; Christine Stroyan and Lizzie Davey for audio recording management; Susan Millership for audio script management; and ID Audio for audio recording and production.

All images are copyright DK. For more information, please visit www.dkimages.com.

WHAT WILL YOU LEARN NEXT?

BOOKS

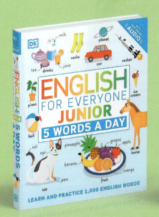
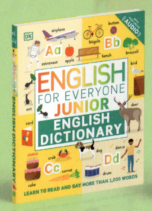

FLASH CARDS